ASATRU FOR I

A Pagan Guide for Heathens to Discovering the Magic of Norse Paganism, Viking Mythology and the Poetic Edda

Melissa Gomes

ASATRU FOR BEGINNERS: A Pagan Guide for Heathens to Discovering the Magic of Norse Paganism, Viking Mythology and the Poetic Edda

by Melissa Gomes

© Copyright 2021 by Melissa Gomes

All Rights Reserved.

No part of this publication may be reproduced, distributed, or transmitted in any form or by any means, including photocopying, recording, or other electronic or mechanical methods, without the prior written permission of the publisher, except in the case of brief quotations embodied in reviews and certain other noncommercial uses permitted by copyright law.

Disclaimer: This book is designed to provide accurate and authoritative information in regard to the subject matter covered. By its sale, neither the publisher nor the author is engaged in rendering psychological or other professional services. If expert assistance or counseling is needed, the services of a competent professional should be sought.

TABLE OF CONTENTS

- TABLE OF CONTENTS 3
- INTRODUCTION 6
- BONUS 1: FREE WORKBOOK - VALUE ~~12.99$~~ 9
- BONUS 2: FREE BOOK – VALUE ~~$14.99~~ 10
- BONUS 3: FREE AUDIO VERSION OF THIS BOOK 11
- GET IN TOUCH! 12
- CHAPTER 1: WHAT IS NORSE PAGANISM? 13
  - CORE BELIEFS AND OTHER IMPORTANT BEINGS 14
- CHAPTER 2: HISTORY OF ASATRU 17
  - THE STONE AGE 18
  - THE BRONZE AGE 19
  - THE CELTIC IRON AGE 20
  - THE ROMAN IRON AGE 21
  - THE MIGRATION ERA 22
  - THE VIKING AGE 24
  - THE REBIRTH OF AN ANCIENT RELIGION 26
- CHAPTER 3: ASATRU AND HEATHENISM 30
  - UNDERSTANDING HEATHENISM AND ASATRU 31
  - PERSPECTIVES ON ASATRU 33
- CHAPTER 4: DEITIES AND OTHER ENTITIES 36
  - AESIR 37
  - VANIR 57
  - JOTNAR 60
- CHAPTER 5: THE CONCEPTS OF WYRD AND ORLOG 63
  - THE IDEAL COMPUTER 66
- CHAPTER 6: GET TO KNOW THE ASATRU AND NORSE SYMBOLS 68
  - YGGDRASIL 68
  - THE HORN OF ODIN (TRIPLE HORN, HORNED TRISKELE) 68
  - VALKNUT 69
  - VEGVISIR 70

    THE NINE WORLDS 70
    HELM OF AWE (AEGISHJALMUR) 71
    JORMUNGANDR 71
    THOR'S HAMMER (MJOLNIR) 72
    RUNES (RUNIC ALPHABET) 72
    CELTIC SHIELD KNOT 73
    TROLL CROSS 73
    THE SOLAR CROSS 74
    HUGIN AND MUNIN 75
    GUNGNIR 75
    SPIRIT SHIP 76
    SLEIPNIR 76
    IRMINSUL 77
    THE WEB OF WYRD 77
    THE MISTRESS OF ANIMALS 78
    NIDSTANG 78
    EINHERJAR 79
    OSEBERG 79
    JULBOCK 79

CHAPTER 7: THE NINE NOBLE VIRTUES 81
    COURAGE 81
    TRUTH 82
    HONOR 83
    FIDELITY 84
    DISCIPLINE 85
    HOSPITALITY 85
    SELF-RELIANCE 86
    INDUSTRIOUSNESS 87
    PERSEVERANCE 88

CONCLUSION 90

CHAPTER 8: COSMOLOGY—THE TREE OF LIFE AND THE NINE WORLDS 93
    YGGDRASIL 93
    THE NINE WORLDS OF ASATRU 94
    INNANGARD AND UTANGARD 103

CHAPTER 9: RUNES, CHARMS, AND MAGIC 107
    RUNE MEANING IN THE ELDER FUTHARK 108
    RUNE CASTING TECHNIQUES 117
    THROWING OR CASTING METHOD 119

4

CHAPTER 10: HEATHEN RITUALS—WHAT DO YOU NEED 121
- Asatru symbol 121
- Fire 122
- Altars 122
- Incantations and Conversations 123
- Location 123
- Blót 124
- Sumble 125
- Create Your Rituals: Four Factors to Consider 126
- Ritual Roles and Ritual Participation 129
- Designing Your Ideal Blót 130
- Kennings, Alliteration, and Bynames 131

CHAPTER 11: HEATHEN HOLIDAYS AND FESTIVALS 134
- Yule or Yuletide – The 12-Day Festival 134
- Disting 135
- Ostara (March 20th–21st) 135
- Walpurgis Night or May Eve (April 30th–May Day) 136
- Midsummer – Summer Solstice (June 20th–21st) 136
- Freyfest or Lammas or Lithasblot (July 31st–August 1st) 137
- Harvestfest or Winter Nights (October 31st) 138

CHAPTER 12: THE CONTEMPORARY ASATRUAR 139
- Follow Asatru in five steps 140
- Getting in touch with fellow Asatruars 143
- Kindred Communities 144

CHAPTER 13: PERFORMING A BLOT 146
- A Communal Blot to Frigga 146
- A Solitary Blot for Frigga 152
- The Hammer Rite 153

WELL DONE! 155

BONUS 1: FREE WORKBOOK - VALUE ~~12.99$~~ 156

BONUS 2: FREE BOOK – VALUE ~~$14.99~~ 157

BONUS 3: FREE AUDIO VERSION OF THIS BOOK 158

INTRODUCTION

I have always been drawn to the mystical world of Norse Mythology and spirituality but was never sure where on Earth I fit in.

After some careful reading of Asatru literature and going through questions like "Who are my ancestors?" I realized that it is not only possible to make it a central part of my life but also an important one for me.

I became an Asatruar after I had been looking for my identity and origins and came across some information about the Norse gods. As soon as I read it, I felt a connection with it. This religion helped me find myself—my true self—when there were no other ways or people out there who seemed to understand.

After nine years of practicing this religion, I felt like it's my duty as a heathen to share some of my knowledge with you so that you can find the same feeling and maybe even your calling as an Asatruar.

During my time as an Asatruar, I have gone through some transformative experiences, both physical and spiritual.

I became more aware of myself and the world around me. The things that I used to think of as "nothing," such as paying attention to the cycles of nature, started making more sense.

I felt like I belonged for the first time in my life and that it was a place where I could be myself without feeling any judgment from others or having shameful thoughts about who I might be.

It's been nine years since I was initiated into this religion, and every day feels like a new adventure, full of challenges and opportunities. I know that you can feel the same as I do.

There are many issues that Asatru solves, from finding a sense of purpose in the world and belonging to being able to live your life according to heathen values.

First is an issue of identity—Who am I? Where do I come from? What are my history and ancestry? By answering these questions, you will find yourself on a path towards discovering your true self. Second is about living one's life according to heathen values such as honor, courage, justice, and hospitality—the things that make up our character. This is achieved by understanding what they mean and incorporating them into daily life so that they become part of us. Finally, it can help you understand yourself better through its teachings so that you can be at peace with yourself as well as with others and the world as a whole.

You might be looking for a religion that is rooted in history as well as the present and can help you uncover yourself. Asatru is a religion that has its roots in Norse mythology, contemporary sources and is alive in the world. In other words, it offers something for everyone with its ancient ideals as well as its new teachings.

I believe that the best way to get people interested in Asatru is by being open and truthful. It's more effective than trying to convince people about our beliefs and their validity or force them into something they don't want.

In this book, I use my own personal stories to share knowledge with you so that you can find the same feeling that I had when I first found it—a place where I belong without any judgment or shame.

I know how hard it is to find oneself and to live one's life according to heathen values. It is my belief that we all have the potential for greatness within us—all we need is an opportunity to fulfill it.

If you don't know where to start or what to do as an Asatruar, then this book will help you find a place where you can feel at home as well as the knowledge that will preserve your heritage for future generations.

This is not only about learning and understanding but also taking action and making those changes in order to live in a world where nature's forces are as relevant as our human ones, as well as finding the inner peace that comes from a sense of harmony.

This book will guide you through the process and will show you how to live in accordance with our religion, as well as ensuring that your family line continues for generations to come.

Treat it as a guide for those who are interested in Asatru without being too academic. It has been written to explain this ancient religion as clearly as possible, avoiding unnecessary complications.

You will find out what it means to be an Asatruar and learn the details of different rituals, as well as find out about all the important deities, symbols, and practices. I believe that this book will help you find your place in this religion.

What's the hurry? There are plenty of people out there who are convinced that they want to learn more but just don't know where to start.

They're looking for someone with a story or guide that reflects their personal experiences and will tell them what it means to be an Asatruar from a simple, non-academic point of view.

Take some time now: read this book in your own way and take action on what you've learned when you feel ready.

Before you do so, please take your time to review the bonuses I've created for you below.

BONUS 1: FREE WORKBOOK - VALUE ~~12.99$~~

To help you take some time for yourself and reflect on what actions to take while reading the book, I have prepared a Free Workbook with some key questions to ask yourself and a To Do List which can help you get deeper into the topic of this book. I hope this helps!

You can find the Free Workbook by visiting

>> https://swiy.io/AsatruWB<<

OR scan the QR Code with your phone's camera

Bonus 2: Free Book – Value $14.99

As a way of saying thank you for downloading this book, I'm offering the eBook *RUNES FOR BEGINNERS A Pagan Guide to Reading and Casting the Elder Futhark Rune Stones for Divination, Norse Magic and Modern Witchcraft* for FREE.

In *Runes for Beginners*, Melissa Gomes reveals some of the most interesting and secret aspects of how to perform Runes Reading and Runes Casting. You will discover new insights into the magical word of Runes and how to link with them.

Click Below for the Free Gift Or Scan the QR Code with your phone

>> https://swiy.io/RunesFree<<

Bonus 3: Free Audio Version of This Book

If you love listening to audiobooks on-the-go or would enjoy a narration as you read along, I have great news for you. You can download the audiobook version of ***Asatru for Beginners*** for FREE just by signing up for a FREE 30-day Audible trial!

Visit the website https://swiy.io/AsatruAudioBook OR scan the QR code with your phone:

Get In Touch!

You'll never find your way without someone to guide you and help you through. I'm here for that!

I have created a Facebook group about **spirituality** where people can get in touch with one another, as well as myself, so we may learn together from each other's knowledge base during our own individual journeys into the unknown realms of life, faith, love. Life is exciting when shared openly!

While you are on your journey of spiritual discovery, join my Facebook group here https://swiy.io/littlespiritualFB or visit my blog at littlespiritual.com/blog to discover more on Spirituality and be part of a growing and thriving community of likeminded people!

Chapter 1: What Is Norse Paganism?

Norse paganism is a religion that originated in Northern Europe. Around the 6th century, this branch of Germanic religion was labeled as Norse paganism, and it spread like wildfire across Denmark and Norway before it reached Sweden by the 8th century. It's popularly referred to as Old Norse Religion, but some scholars say this term may be misleading because many other cultures outside Scandinavia share similar practices with much older roots than even what we call "Norse."

It was, in fact, the most prevalent form of Germanic religion followed by the Anglo-Saxons. Norse paganism was a polytheistic religion, meaning that they had many gods and goddesses, with Odin as their chief deity. Norse paganism is also famous for its use of the runes in divination. In fact, they were the first people to use runes as a writing system.

There are many practices of Norse paganism that have survived in modern-day Scandinavian culture, such as Yule—or Christmas—and Jolablot, which is like our Easter celebration.

Norse paganism was at its peak during the Viking Age, and it was widespread throughout the Scandinavian countries.

The most famous Norse pagan practice is called seidr or Odinism. It's a type of sorcery that means that they had many gods and goddesses; their chief deity was Odin, who used runes to divine information for people; hence, the reason this magical activity has survived until modern day.

The Norse gods are the major deities in Scandinavian paganism, also known as Asatru. They were worshiped by a variety of people for the different domains they owned and represented. Some examples include Odin (chief deity), Thor, Freya, and Loki to name a few.

CORE BELIEFS AND OTHER IMPORTANT BEINGS

Norse paganism teaches the idea of a merciful and all-powerful god, Odin, who is responsible for everything in existence. All other gods are either his children or his agents of creation. The Norse believed in multiple worlds, including one we live in—Midgard—which they thought was surrounded by an ocean with another world above it called Asgard, home of the gods and goddesses like Valhalla (warriors' hall).

Most people are familiar with Odin. But did you know that there was also another group of beings that influenced life on Earth? The Norns were three supernatural female figures credited for shaping destiny through their weaving; these ladies have been known since time immemorial by many names, including Urda, Verdandi, and Skulda. They live at the foot of Yggdrasil, where they take water from Hvergelmir (the boiling spring) that flows into Mimir's well near Niflheim—an important location in controlling access between realms.

Another being described in Norse mythology is the vaettir. It is important to note that these are not elves but have different characteristics and habits than the Aesir or Vanir gods. The vaettir are represented in Norse mythology as spirits, and the term can be used to represent any kind of supernatural creature that is not Aesir or Vanir.

The importance of the vaettir lies in their ability to interact with humans through seidr, a form of sorcery that was also practiced by some women and men which could be used for good or bad purposes. Seidr is rooted deeply in Norse culture; it has been described as "the Nordic shamanic technique" and may have had an influence on pre-Christian Anglo-Saxon witchcraft. The magic associated with this practice can take many forms, including healing people from disease or injury and hexing one's enemies—"wolf spells" were often casted using a combination of both black arts and white charms against those who would harm other family members or oneself. The use of magic for both good and evil purposes was not limited to seidr, nor did it only belong to the realm of women; in particular, men used sorcery for healing before battle as well.

A third group of beings in Norse mythology is dwarves; they are also considered supernatural figures because their lifespan exceeds mortals. They live underground beneath volcanoes where they craft precious metals like gold for humans.

The final group is jotnar, which includes giants such as the Midgard serpent Jormungandr and a fierce woman named Hela who presides over those souls deemed unworthy at death (Hela does not rule Valhalla). She rules from Niflheim, now located on Earth rather than with her brother Loki under Asgard after causing Ragnarok.

The Norse gods are a fascinating bunch. They're all about war, love, and death with some epic power struggles between them that make for great stories to tell around the campfire.

Norse mythology consists of many tales concerning heroes who fought against evil forces in order to restore peace or stability on Earth among other things, like maintaining natural cycles such as day/night, winter/summer, etc. Justice was served oftentimes by having battles, which were always presided over by one god acting as judge while another acted out both sides so they could not be biased towards either party even though it would seem odd looking at this from today's perspective where everyone is "equal."

The ancient world was full of gods, goddesses, and spirits. The Vanir were equivalent to nature deities, while the Aesir ruled over a more disciplined set of rules.

In Norse mythology, there are two different types of beings: those belonging to the Aesir tribe or in some cases just called "gods," which includes Odin, Frigga, Thor, Baldr, and Tyr. The other tribe is known as Vanir.

The Vanir are not enemies to the Aesir, but they do have different approaches to life that can be seen with Freya, whose approach to life is more liberated than Frigga, Odin's wife. So, it is interesting how these two groups would mingle in some cases, and they would fight in others.

This is why it is important to know the difference between these two groups of beings, because they are not simply different but their approaches to life and what they value most are also very much so.

Another key belief in Norse paganism is the idea of balance. The Norse people believed that there was a constant struggle between the forces of good and evil; for example, Odin is both god of war and wisdom. This idea of balance is also seen with the connection of love and war, where warriors would have a lover that they had to leave behind when going into battle.

Chapter 2: History Of Asatru

Asatru, which means "faith in the Aesir (gods)," is a modern word that Danish researchers used in the 19th century to refer to Scandinavia's pre-Christian religion. The name of this faith comes from long ago, when people believed many gods and goddesses were walking around on Earth with humans. Unfortunately, not much has been passed down about how these ancient religions would have looked or functioned. However, we do know what they did for their rituals: sacrifice livestock like cows as appeasement offerings to various deities depending on region, climate, etc., always involving fire somehow, as it has been integral throughout history due to its purifying powers.

The Swedish, Danish, and Norwegian all pronounce the word differently. The Icelandic pronunciation is phonetically *ow-sa-troo* with a "w" sound like in English words such as work or would.

People who believe in the Norse gods refer to themselves as Asatruars, but there are a variety of ways that they go about it. Some people avoid using "Asatru" altogether and just call themselves heathens instead—which may have something to do with them not wanting their god's name revealed easily or for some other reason entirely.

A heathen originally meant a person who was not educated or noble. The word has evolved to mean someone who is non-Christian and doesn't believe in any gods. Religions like Buddhism don't count as "heathens."

Originally meaning one without privilege, today's definition of heathen comes from an old Anglo-Saxon root that literally means "of the common people."

The Norse gods are making a big comeback in the modern world. In fact, many believers in these ancient deities simply call themselves "heathens" as an act of defiance against Christianity and its followers.

The recent rise in heathenism is due in part to people's desire for something more authentic than what mainstream religion offers, but it also stems from their unwillingness to be judged or silenced by Christian communities who stereotype them negatively based solely on this belief system.

THE STONE AGE

The thousand-year-old Norse religion of Asatru was a powerful blend of shamanistic and animist beliefs that had evolved to include worshiping ancestors. This led many followers in the Stone Age to believe their shamans could not only communicate with nature and ancestral spirits but also control them, for good or evil. Asatru was a shamanistic religion that focused on communicating with nature spirits and ancestors during the Stone Age.

There is no evidence of Asatru in Scandinavia before the Stone Age. However, there are indications that some aspects may date back to at least as early as 3000 BCE. In particular, Norse mythology has many references to natural forces beyond human control, such as storms or fire, which likely would have been interpreted by people living during this period through shamanistic beliefs.

Shamans perform many rituals based on their belief in these spirits, including the use of charms.

Shamanistic practices were key to Asatru for a long time and still are today, with some practitioners following them more than others.

This is seen as either an inherited survival from ancient times or simply reflecting our need to reconnect with nature's power.

THE BRONZE AGE

We refer to the Bronze Age as Asatru's first period of historical relevance.

The Bronze Age is about the time when humans discovered how to extract and smelt metals, including copper, which became a key element in early Asatru ritual tools such as hammers and axes.

During this age, Asatru really began to take shape from an idea into a religion with its practices for believers to follow.

Several ancient texts were written by people living in Scandinavia at this time, looking back on their beliefs long after they died out. These are known as the Eddas, but they only tell one side of the story.

The other part of the story is found in archeological finds.

One of the most important Asatru sites ever found is a place called Maeshowe in Scotland. It was built about 2500 years ago with all these curious carvings that are symbolic of Asatru, like spirals and runes on the outside walls and inside as well.

What's really interesting is what lies beneath this site: coffins lined up one after another, filled with the skeletons of people who died near or around the time it was created. This means they were buried there for some spiritual reason.

Asatru in the Bronze Age was characterized by an increased focus on warfare, including farming and trade. In addition to worshiping Aesir gods, people would have revered Vanir deities too. The Vanir were associated with fertility, whereas the Aesir represented war and death.

During this time, a belief system known as seidr (a type of Norse shamanism) developed, which involved shapeshifting into an animal form to communicate with spirits or cast healing spells on sick humans. This is similar to what many people would call "animal magic" today, although it was much more specifically related to these practices during the Bronze Age than it is now.

Tacitus mentioned the Asatruar in his writings. The Aesir were thought to be "gods of light," while the Vanir deities were considered "gods of darkness."

Tacitus also mentioned that Asatruars worshiped the god Thor and sacrificed animals as offerings to him.

The Celtic Iron Age

The Celtic culture was present in Scandinavia for centuries before the Iron Age, and it had a lasting impact on Scandinavian religion. The Gundestrup cauldron is one of many artifacts that highlight this cultural exchange, depicting gods like Cernunnos with his horns and Taranis wielding thunderbolts as weapons. Morgana may also be depicted among these Celtic deities, since she has been noted to have existed prior to the Roman invasions of France, where her worship sites were found by archeologists.

The Cimbri, Ambrones, and Teutons were tribes from the north that invaded Rome from 105 to 101 BCE. All three are believed by historians today to have originated in Scandinavia, with the name "Cimbrian" being later used for an area on the Jutland Peninsula, which is now known as Denmark's southernmost point. It was these people who first inhabited this peninsula before it came into Roman hands, but their origins remain somewhat unclear according to some scholars based partly on existing archeological evidence at various sites around Europe—thanks largely in part to living outside of Rome throughout most if not all of their history up until then.

The Romans had to fight a war with the Germanic-speaking Cimbri and Teutons. The first evidence of these people in Europe is from Roman literature, which was around 170 BCE, during Rome's last decade before its fall. In this period, both humans and animals were sacrificed by the Germans in some kind of rite or ceremony—a custom seen throughout Scandinavia at the same time in history, according to archeological findings.

THE ROMAN IRON AGE

The Germanic people have a long and fascinating history. They first appeared in literature during the time of Julius Caesar's writings on his conquest of Gaul, but they were not given much attention until Tacitus wrote about them in more detail from 98 CE onward. Germania was the name given by the Romans to their territory north of the Rhine, and it became their own name. In fact, Tacitus mentioned that these people had female leaders who could perform witchcraft—we know this because he included some interesting aspects, such as how they chose witches by testing if they would float when thrown into water.

Tacitus had an extensive knowledge of the Germanic people and their gods, but he gave them Latin names. One such god is Mercury (Odin), who was worshiped for his swiftness in battle. Another popular deity among the Germans was Jupiter or Thor as known by Norsemen, chosen by warriors with a thirst for bloodshed on battlefields beyond counting. Tacitus also described Nerthus being worshiped during pre-Christian times when she took over after Odin became unpopular because he was associated with warring ways that disturbed agricultural pursuits.

Tacitus, one of the most notable Roman historians, wrote about how, during his time in Germania, they would sacrifice humans to the lakes. There have been many findings that show people were sacrificed for ritual purposes and even more finds from around Europe after he mentioned it. Bog bodies are well-preserved human bodies with skin, hair, and teeth left intact by their long stay in oxygen-free sludge at the bottom of ancient lakes.

During Tacitus' visit to Germany (98 CE), sacrifices involving individuals being thrown into a lake were a common practice among tribes living near these natural pools or bogs. However, this topic has sparked endless debate over whether this gruesome act is fact or fiction, since little evidence supporting such claims was found in modern times.

THE MIGRATION ERA

This was an era in which Asatru was probably practiced widely. The Migration Era started around 300 CE when people from Scandinavia migrated to other parts of Europe and created settlements, including Iceland. It can be assumed that these settlers brought their religion with them and started practicing it again wherever they went, making Asatru one of many religions being practiced during this time. There are no specific written records detailing what type of Asatru practice existed at this point because there were few literate cultures living at the same time as those migrating groups moving through Europe, but we do know for certain that Christianity had become widespread by then, so it may well have come into contact with them.

In 500 CE, Germanic peoples migrated from northern Germany, Scandinavia, and the coastal regions of modern-day Poland. The Migration Era is a time of great mystery as to what occurred in those tumultuous centuries and has been lost, but we know that nomadic tribes were moving into new territories with different cultures and customs than theirs.

There were many migrations in 500 CE by people living close to Northern Europe who had not yet found ways or groups willing enough to expand southward following barbarian invasions. So, these expansions could be seen as an upheaval caused by a lack of resources rather than a need for space, because they had already inhabited most of the available areas on Earth at this point in history.

The Anglo-Saxons migrated to Britain and founded England. They named it after their ancestors' homeland, but they were not bound by what was left behind in the old country; instead, these warriors sought new opportunities on this island from which we now derive our name: "Anglo" or angle, which is an Old English word meaning bend or corner. The Franks established France as a powerful kingdom.

The Goths and Heruli claimed to have originated in a land called "Thule," which is now known as Scandinavia by some scholars.

The Greco-Roman name for what we know today as Scandinavia translates to "the country of dark forests." So, it's no surprise why these two tribes would claim this area as their own homeland, based on its ancient roots.

The Romans had many different impacts on the Scandinavian people. They were able to learn from them and, in turn, influenced their society as well by teaching Roman customs such as military tactics and art techniques like mosaics.

The Migration Period was an interesting time for both Scandinavia and Rome because it allowed both people to grow while learning about each other's cultures.

The Romans brought much to the Scandinavian people, and not just their customs. They also gave them a taste for drinking wine and introduced an improved type of plow that could cut through clay soil with ease—it was called the Roman wheeled plow.

Starting around 300 CE, the Germanic tribes in south-central Europe began to convert heavily to Christianity. After centuries of tribal warfare during which they were constantly at odds with one another over land and money, these groups found that their new religion provided a unifying thread and strong moral guidance on what was right or wrong.

THE VIKING AGE

The Viking Age began with Charlemagne's invasion of the Frankish kingdom. The king conquered his way through Europe and claimed new lands, giving him control over much of Western Europe. It was during this time that the Vikings made their mark on history for the first time in 793 CE when they attacked Saint Cuthbert's monastery at Lindisfarne off England's coast, for reasons still unclear to this day. The Norsemen left not one stone unturned and pillaged everything from food stocks to relics like books and crucifixes. Those unfortunate enough to be caught up in these raids had little hope of escape; most met grisly ends by sword or axe, while others were traded into slavery among the Nordic tribes across Europe, where many died due to the harsh conditions.

Due to a lack of written records from that time period, historians are still debating what exactly led hundreds of Scandinavian men and women on raids as far away as Constantinople (modern-day Istanbul). Some speculate they were pushed out by pressure from other Nordic tribes or looking for more land; others believe they wanted revenge against Christianity after their native gods failed them during times when crops had perished.

The Vikings evolved into raiders, invaders, and traders. They traded with the Byzantine Empire in Constantinople and eventually began to sail westward into uncharted territory.

Following their conversion to Christianity, these groups grew tired of tribal warfare that took away time spent on other activities such as farming or family life. As a result, they found that their new religion provided both moral guidance on right and wrong and a unifying thread among them, which helped bring peace between all those who had converted. In fact, this unified feeling was so strong that it caused many tribes in southern Europe to become Christians.

The Vikings were a fierce and war-loving people. They believed that they would be taken to Valhalla after death, where all the slain warriors had been brought together for eternity with Odin and Frigga—two of their gods who sacrificed themselves at Ragnarok in order to allow new life on Earth.

The most interesting descriptions of the Viking Age religion come from Muslim emissaries Ahmad Ibn Fadlan and Yaqub Al-Tartushi, both Arab writers living among groups of Norsemen or North Africans around 900 CE. They have given us a glimpse into how they worshiped deities like Odin in stories full of dragons, giants, witches, and witchcraft. This ancient culture appears to have something for everyone: adventure seekers who enjoy mythical creatures; those interested in ritualistic practices such as seidr or rune reading; individuals seeking spiritual enlightenment while attempting to better understand oneself through self-reflection techniques such as meditation—all of these things were part of the Vikings' lives.

Throughout this period, Norsemen worshiped various pagan gods, who controlled natural phenomena such as thunderstorms, fertility and childbirth, battles, death, and so on. This practice continued into Christianity, with many Nordic people erecting monuments to these pagan gods all across their homeland, often with Christian inscriptions, with Thor, Uller, and Tyr all widely worshiped.

The way the places dedicated to deities are spread out indicates a great deal of diversity in pre-Christian Scandinavian worship. According to research, there were at least 30 different gods with their own individual stories and characteristics worshiped across Scandinavia before Christianity introduced its standardized religion. This means that within this region alone, you can find many strange names that originate from various religions.

The multiplicity of these ancient beliefs is evident even today: archeologists have discovered multiple Viking sites with altars erected by followers who prayed specifically to Odin, Frigga, and Freya, among others.

The Viking Age was a time of great change, and with that came an opportunity for many people to explore new ideas. One topic in particular is what the Vikings believed about their gods. Archeological finds from this period can help us understand how these beliefs developed over time as well as which deities were favored by different groups or individuals at certain periods during history.

Many archeological findings have been uncovered due to technological advances in recent centuries, such as rune stones, coins, jewelry-making equipment, and everyday objects like pottery shards or kitchenware found buried on ancient farms near big cities throughout Scandinavia. These items give historians information related not only to human activity but also to religious practices among the early Scandinavian peoples who lived there more than a millennia ago.

The Rebirth Of An Ancient Religion

For centuries, scholars and enthusiasts alike have been fascinated by the ancient Eddic poems. These Icelandic epics comprised myths that were passed down orally for generations before their written versions sometime around 1200 CE. The most famous poets of these tales are Snorri Sturluson and Sturla Throddarson, who lived between 1103 and 1184 CE.

In 1643, Bishop Brynjolfr Sveinsson found a manuscript containing Eddic poems in Skalholt. He rediscovered some of these manuscripts after a long time, and during his search, he ran into something amazing: sagas from Iceland's ancient past! These sagas were stories about traditions and beliefs before Christianity came to Scandinavia. The content included magic spells for healing illnesses and executions by burning at the stake or drowning, which became popular when paganism was still widely practiced.

The first Icelandic historian, Saemundr Inn Frodi (1056 to 1133 CE), is believed by some scholars of the time to be the author and originator of The Prose Edda. Although there are no solid sources that can confirm this claim, similar prose found in his writing supports it, as well as how he was known for being a wise man who often studied ancient texts from various cultures.

The accepted wisdom is that Saemundr wrote the poems in this collection. However, it has been discovered recently by a scholar from Iceland University that he could not have written these works because we now know they were authored over 70 years after his death in 1205 CE.

Neo-paganism emerged in the 19th century, but it's been speculated that there were traces of these tendencies before then. With an uptick in pagan worship and beliefs following World War I, many people began to identify as Neo-pagans as a result of their practices or beliefs.

Neo-paganism first appeared around 1819, with interest originating in Iceland around 1780, when Christianity was still relatively new on the island, which makes sense given that Norse mythology is one form of Neo-pagan belief system. It wasn't until after WWI that devout followers started identifying themselves as such while practicing more modern forms, like Wicca, which came about in 1939 by Gerald Gardner, who would go on to attract converts through his writings.

The 1950s saw a rise in the popularity of witchcraft, specifically Wicca. This branch is often seen as providing women with an empowering medium for self-expression and spirituality while simultaneously reclaiming their place at higher levels of society that were previously denied to them.

Witchcraft has evolved over hundreds, if not thousands, of years, so it's no surprise that modern witches draw inspiration from sources other than traditional European folk magic, such as African traditions like Vodun or various Native American practices like smudging (an ancient purification ceremony involving the burning of aromatic resins).

Wicca's influence on the Norse religion has been seen for decades now. In 1994, many Asatruars started to feel that they needed a stronger connection with their roots and began looking back at ancient sources of information that had not yet been tainted by Wiccan or Celtic influences.

Many people were raised in pagan religions other than Asatru during this time (Wiccans being one such group), but they soon found themselves drawn to it because its beliefs were so closely aligned with what we know today about the pre-Christian Nordic traditions.

In contrast to the traditional Norsemen, modern urban Asatruars have a more individualistic view of life; they are less concerned about being part of an order or society.

The modern Asatruar is connected to the natural world in ways that many people can't even imagine. They make sure they are fully grounded and centered before entering their home, as it's one of the most common places where negative energy gathers.

The typical modern Asatruar has a strong connection with nature; so much more than what you would find among those who have never experienced the true wilderness firsthand. When coming into your own abode, for example—which happens to be one of the areas ripe with negativity—these individuals will often take time beforehand, just being outside or sitting on grass or dirt until completely relaxed and comfortable enough to enter again without feeling drained by all that comes at them internally.

Chapter 3: Asatru And Heathenism

For many Asatruar, there is no single route to being heathen. Some people focus on the gods of war (Aesir) while others may revere the goddesses of love and fertility (Vanir). Others find it most important to honor their ancestors and interact with spirits in nature.

For those who follow Asatru, this religion can be practiced in wildly different ways depending on what a person values more: interacting with deities such as Odin and Thor? Honoring your ancestral lineages through rituals like seidr? Connecting intimately with nature's spirit by animal sacrifice for instance?

There are many ways to heathenism, but at the heart of it all is a deep and abiding respect for nature. Those who worship Aesir put their faith in mighty gods like Thor or Loki while those who favor Vanir revere Freya or Freyr. Ancestors and spirits hold special meaning too, as they remind us that there will always be someone watching over our loved ones even after death, waiting in another world where we can find them again someday.

Heathens can choose to worship one of the gods, all of them, or none at all. Some are more focused on ancestors and spirits, while others put their faith in a specific god such as Thor, who is known for his strong sense of justice.

Heathens have many ways they can practice heathenry; some people focus heavily on Odinism where there's an emphasis placed upon Norse traditions like honoring our family members with rituals like funerals, but it doesn't require you to be pagan, which means that someone may not even believe in any spirituality outside Christianity yet still wishes to honor those lost through traditional rites without converting into another religion.

Some Americans find that they have ancestral ties to Northern Europe, so it's no surprise that many are attracted to Asatru and heathenry. Because of this strong connection with their ancestors' homeland, these individuals often want to forge a new path for themselves using what knowledge is available about the culture from where their family came from.

In Europe, many different groups identify as Asatru and heathens who specifically worship the Norse gods.

Some of the main ones in Europe, and in the world are

- *Ásatrúarfélagid (Iceland)*
- *The Odinic Rite (UK)*
- *The Troth (USA, Canada, and New Zealand)*
- *The Ring of Troth/The Council of Australian Heathens Ltd (Australia)*
- *Asatru Society Icelanders for Progressive Christianity in Reykjavík, Islandsfelagid/Öskjuhlið (Church)*
- *Icelandic Pagan Association/Félag Pagansins (Pagan Society)*
- *Forn Siðr (Swedish organization for heathens who follow the old Norse religion and live according to its customs)*
- *Yggdrasil's Wreath (American organization that promotes Asatru as a faith based on scholarship and research)*

UNDERSTANDING HEATHENISM AND ASATRU

Paganism refers to several belief systems with no Biblical basis and is mostly centered on polytheism and pantheism, such as the ancient Celtic and Slavic religions. Another more recent movement is Dianic Wicca, whose followers—called "witches"—worship the Goddess and other female deities like Freya, Hecate, and Artemis. The entire Norse pantheon is revered in Germanic heathenism, especially Odin and Frigga, who were influential in mythology, with Thor being the most popular. Still, modern-day Asatru prefers the Icelandic Aesir gods over the others.

Asatru adherents are aware of and believe in the Vanir gods, stemming from Norse paganism. However, they do not discuss or worship any other deities but those of the Aesir tribe. This might be due to minimal engagement between these lesser-known figures and Asatru followers who only focus on the beliefs set by the Aesir tribes. Since many devout members adhere to very structured rules on what's expected from them as participants, this can lead to an entire community following suit, which could be seen as more formal than most traditions based around religious faith today.

Ancient Norse religion, now also known as heathenism and Asatru, is at the forefront of a modern movement seeking small-scale communities that are self-sufficient in their respective traditions—varying by region and family upbringing—for their purposes. Heathenism and Asatru have a documented history dating back to the Iron Age, with beliefs rooted in Germanic paganism. Although the meaning of "heathen" has changed over time, it currently describes one who believes in multiple gods or divine beings but does not identify with any particular religion themselves. Consequentially, most believers prefer "Asatru" due to its less negative connotations for those who don't understand its meaning.

If one is looking for a tolerant religion or does not impose anything on its believers to become part of the community, Asatru might be one of the best bets.

An essential aspect in understanding Asatru is that missionary or proselytizing events are not conducted. People are welcome to join this community if they wish, but there is no requirement for conversion to a Heathen. Conversion should be due to the calling of one's inner voice and destiny towards this way of life.

Perspectives On Asatru

The modern Asatru/Heathenism community is divided into three camps: Universalism, Folkism, and Tribalism. The first two perspectives are the most important, while the third takes a middle-ground approach.

Universalism

For Asatru, universalism is understanding Asatru not as a religion but carries the same relevance as Judaism and Christianity. It's about acceptance of all religious beliefs, no matter what they may be.

This belief system does not exclude anyone who wishes to partake in it nor allow any person or group to claim sole ownership over Asatru because it was founded on universalism—making it possible for people from other faiths to come into Asatru with open arms.

One of the primary arguments against Asatru Universalism is that it falls short in honoring its own culture and history.

One of the major criticisms levied on Asatru Universalism, often by those who are not satisfied with its openness to other cultures, is that this tradition may be too open-minded because there are people who want their religion to have a unique identity rather than being part of an overarching global one.

Folkism

Asatru Folkism believes that only North European ancestry should be admitted to the religion, an ethnic tradition. Folkism believes that ethnic religions connect followers to their local landscape, bloodlines, ancestors, and practices. As a result, outsiders will struggle to relate to ethnic elements, and the religion will lose its authenticity.

In contrast to other folkish groups that are very exclusionary, the Asatru Association welcomes all who want to enter their doors (even if they have not experienced a heathen lifestyle before), so long as they show an interest in learning about Asatru.

Folkists are frequently labeled as white supremacists because they would have difficulty accepting newcomers with no North European roots in Asatru. Still, they insist that their position is not one of supremacy but of a strong desire to honor their ancestors.

Opponents of Folkism also make a counter-argument in their favor. They cite the Eddas and other Norse mythology and legends for the existence of several non-Norse people and characters. Non-Norse characters also took part in ceremonies and rituals.

In addition, a lot of people who oppose Folkism also point out that it's unjust to discriminate against someone for something they can't change.

Norse people who migrated to other areas, on the other hand, embraced and assimilated the cultures and customs of those places. Despite these arguments, Folkism maintains its philosophy of refusing to accept everyone into the Asatru fold.

TRIBALISM

Folkism and Universalism are at opposite extremities of the Asatru spectrum, while Tribalism adherents are in the center.

It's a little confusing, but tribalism is between folkism and universalism. It has some of the themes that universalism has, such as equality and civil rights, but it also has some ideals similar to folkism. Folkism and tribalism have many similarities, including the belief in the importance of people who share a common heritage or history.

Asatru Tribalism recognizes and embraces the Folkism view that being an Asatru requires a deep connection to and feeling for Norse culture. Adherence to these beliefs at any level is insufficient; one must have a strong, personal connection with these beliefs to be considered true followers of the faith. Also, to become an Asatru Tribalist, one must either have Norse/Germanic heritage or been adopted and taken the oath to the community.

Whatever viewpoint picked, keep in mind that the Nordic people place high importance on courage, honor, liberty, individuality, and progress. Furthermore, those who feel drawn to the Asatru path will only be able to experience the belief system in the present. As a result, it is difficult to follow the Old Norse religion in the way it was practiced during the Viking Age.

What matters the most is having a strong connection to Asatru. It necessitates dedication and should go beyond simply studying Odin, Thor, and others. Wearing a replica of Thor's hammer around one's neck is not enough. One will have to learn how to live a real Norse pagan life.

Chapter 4: Deities And Other Entities

This chapter will discuss the main gods and goddesses in Asatru, together with other important beings worth knowing.

It's worth noting that Asatruars regard their gods as individual entities with distinct characteristics. As a result, Asatru has no all-encompassing concept of a "Great Goddess/God." Each deity is unique and should be treated as such.

Norse mythological beings have various names. Asatruars worship the Norse pantheon and incorporate different Germanic gods, such as Eostre and Seaxnot, into their practices.

The gods listed in Snorri's Edda and the Eddic poems make up a small part of the overall number of deities and entities worshipped by heathens. The Edda is a book of lore and has only about 100 gods. But if you count all the various lesser deities, then there could be as many as 1,000 different entities to worship under its cover.

Heathens, like polytheists, don't always worship a single deity. Sometimes, they add deities from different religions if there are reasons for it, such as living where a certain religion is followed or their lineage in other traditions.

The gods of polytheistic cultures have been around for as long as we can remember. In the past, there were even people with entirely different religions than what we practice in our society today. For example, many Germanic tribes worshiped Egyptian Isis or Middle Eastern Dionysus instead of Jesus Christ and other divinities prevalent in Western culture nowadays (but note that not all Germans will give up their own beliefs to follow these

Western cultures theologies). The same groups also worshiped Persian Mithras rather than Shiva because they thought he was more powerful when it came to fighting against evil forces within this world. But eventually, both died out from lack of popularity over time. Finnish and Sámi beings, like in Celtic traditions, have many similarities with the Norse.

AESIR

The gods and goddesses of the Aesir represent knowledge, wisdom, magic, and wonder. The Vanir presided over fertility before their stronger counterparts conquered them in a long-ago battle for power.

The Viking gods of Norse mythology are famous for their heroic deeds and fighting spirit, but they weren't always at odds with one another. After the Aesir tribe started a war against the Vanir—opposing deities in Scandinavian folklore—an agreement was reached to negotiate peace terms after hostilities ceased. "Hostages" from both tribes were returned to their camps to help foster harmony as well as promote cooperation among all parties involved.

ODIN

Odin is a well-known god revered by many Asatruars. Many people refer to him as "the All-Father." Although this is a misinterpretation of his true character in the Edda, Snorri was credited with portraying Odin effectively—the heathen equivalent of the Christian God.

Norsemen worshipped Odin as their highest god. He was the patriarch of this tribe and the most adored among the immortals. As the war god, he would ride his horse Sleipnir into battle to inspire awe in others. He also performed well as an accomplished poet who is said to have written much poetry about death that still survives today. His ring Draupnir, which produces eight new rings for every nine already created, represents his magical ability: one of many attributes possessed by Odin.

Odin is one of the most intriguing and complex Norse gods. He has many different names, all with meanings that seem to fit his personality. For example, he's known as "Master of Fury" in English because he was a fierce god who often rode around on Sleipnir wielding Gungnir. This spear would either make things sprout or wither away depending on how it struck while guided by runes carved onto each nailhead.

Odin, as the god of wisdom and knowledge, set out on an endless quest for enlightenment. His power was comparable to that of a never-ending storm; he pursued learning until it consumed his entire self. Odin's gaze would never stray from knowledge and wisdom; his eyes were always scanning the horizon for new information he could use against Ragnarok to save humanity once again.

Odin's thirst for knowledge was so strong that he willingly sacrificed his eyes to see the cosmos more clearly. He hung from Yggdrasil, learning what he could before returning with runes due to this preternatural accomplishment. Odin never stopped chasing something new and exciting to know about. Thanks to this mindset, we have come closer than ever to understanding some of our universe's great mysteries.

THOR

Thor was the most famous son of Odin and his mother, Jord. He defended people from all realms, wielding Mjolnir—a tremendous hammer that could emit lightning bolts. Thor's bravery is unmatched in many legends; he always does what is right for himself and those around him, making him an incredible healer with great abilities beyond compare!

Thor was the ideal god, and every human fighter aspired to be like him. Odin bestowed storm, wind, and air powers upon him, making him unstoppable in a battle against any opponent. His hammer had enough power to destroy mountains with a single strike!

His steadfast sense of honor and bravery was unmatched; when he wore his belt, Megingjard—gifted to him by his mother as a sign that she would always watch over her son with pride—his power would double.

The Mjolnir is Thor's most famous weapon, and he never leaves without it. The spark of thunder burns brightly in his heart while the power of lightning courses through him. But like all weapons, it's not just a tool for combat; when wielded by an honorable man, it protects against evil forces that threaten Asgard as well.

Thor has many enemies, but none is more powerful than the Jormungandr. This giant snake bites and constricts its prey like no other creature on Earth can. In the end, when Ragnarok comes to pass (the destruction of all things), only one being will have enough power to slay this mighty serpent: Thor himself. Despite this, Jormungandr is said to have killed Thor in Ragnarok.

TYR

Tyr is a warrior willing to give up his arm for the good of humanity. Tyr is a warrior deity who embodied the ultimate sacrifice by giving his hand to Fenrir. He exemplifies ideals such as honor, courage, and sacrifice; he has made significant sacrifices so that others can live peacefully and fearlessly in their own homes. He always bravely fights even if the odds are against him - because it's not about winning or losing but doing everything as best you can while upholding your beliefs.

HEIMDALL

Heimdall is a handsome Norse god with white skin. He is also one of Odin's sons and is known for his loyal skills. He sat on top of Bifrost, a celestial rainbow bridge that connected all realms in the universe to Asgard. There were two things necessary for him to keep watching: his eyes and his spear, Gungnir.

The gods of Asgard were safe from harm because the bridge that connected them to Midgard was guarded by Heimdall, the god who never slept.

Heimdall has a dwelling on top called Himinbjorg or Sky Cliffs. He doesn't require much sleep, so he is always vigilant about protecting his world from intruders like Loki.

He spends all day atop his bridge where not even Loki can find him out for an easy attack because he's watching every corner with unwavering eyes.

His vision is so good that he can see things hundreds of kilometers away at any time of day or night. He's been known to use this power for spying, but his main goal in life is simply sightseeing and exploration.

When he sees danger approaching Asgard, his horn – Gjallarhorn - sounds the alert.

With a bright, full moon shining in the sky and stars sparkling like diamonds on black velvet, Heimdall felt blessed to be living out his final days atop of the Bifrost.

Baldr

Odin and Frigga had a son named Baldr. He was considered the fairest of all gods with his luminous skin. He lived between Heaven and Earth as he embodied both life and death with his immortal nature. Despite this, he was murdered through deception using mistletoe, which had surrounded him from birth until his death.

Some people have interpreted Baldr as a sun god or even Christ-like. But this understanding was not part of his original story and can still have negative consequences for modern practitioners who want to honor him as they should. The god associated with sunshine is Sol; her name means "sun" itself!

Due to these late 19th century interpretations by researchers, he's as misunderstood in modern Asatru as Odin himself - an unjust fate for someone so kind-hearted and loved among his kinfolks.

When he was killed, it brought about the destruction of everything; his death caused so much immeasurable sorrow.

Baldr's myth has nothing in common with Christ, God's son who suffered for our sins. The story goes like this: when he died from Loki's trickery, everyone suffered as they saw their world crumble before them - his absence left such an emptiness inside all those around him, not even Odin could fill it up again.

This misinterpretation happened because scholars in the 19th century didn't comprehend the difference between Christian and non-Christian myths.

Baldr was a god among the gods. Handsome and easy-going, he won the hearts of everyone around him effortlessly. And so, when he began having visions about his death that would take place in Ragnarok by being pierced with arrows from Loki's bow, Frigga traveled across the cosmos to secure pledges not to harm or kill her son.

The gods were bored and wanted to test their new toy. They tossed objects at him, such as thunderbolts, the sun's rays, lightning bolts. But nothing breached his skin. His mother made a minor blunder when she didn't include mistletoe on her list of things that would be too small to damage her son - but it was enough for Loki!

Loki was aware of this, so he gave Hod (or Hodr, the blind god) a sprig of mistletoe and instructed him to toss it at Baldr, as the other gods had done. He died when this little mistletoe touched his body.

Loki

This nefarious god was also a shapeshifter. He can morph into a variety of animal forms. Loki is traditionally described as a fire warrior. In his descriptions as an indispensable companion, a lethal master, and an untrustworthy servant, the fire components are depicted. Loki was a god who could cause a lot of havoc.

A trickster, Loki is always up to no good. He can be either a helper or an enemy depending on his mood at the time - and he changes it often! Known for bestowing gifts in the areas of speech, hearing, sight, and appearance, what's not so great about this? Because his intentions are never pure, these gifts may come with a catch, such as a betrayal by friends or enemies alike.

He has a habit of causing trouble for the gods and goddesses. Despite this, especially when they are in need, he will come to save other gods from their troubles. Although his pranks can be seriously malicious and cause havoc among those who live on Asgard, it only takes one good deed before everything goes back to normal. Many of the gods' famed belongings, such as Odin's Sleipnir and Draupnir, and Thor's Mjolnir, were brought to them by Loki.

Loki is one of the gods who is misrepresented, misread, and misunderstood. The misunderstanding around Loki stems from a literal interpretation with no critical insight into Snorri's Edda, much like misunderstandings about Odin or Baldr.

In Snorri's Edda, Odin is portrayed as a divine figure, Baldr as Jesus, Frigga as Mary, and Loki as Judas. This could have been due to Snorri's desire to present Norse mythology in an interesting way to the Christians of his time by paralleling it with their mythology. The problem now is that current Asatruars, who read the old legends as "lore" and "scripture," are unaware of the backstory.

FORSETI

Forseti, the god of justice, is the son of Baldr and Nanna. He resides in Glitnir Palace, which stands as a court for all legal problems where red gold pillars are crowned with silver roofs.

He is one of the twelve major gods but does not appear in any of the surviving myths. A lesser-known deity within Norse mythology, Forseti has been noted for his kindness and fairness, which he uses to resolve arguments with other deities, often seeking revenge against each other instead. He's the Scandinavian equivalent of a lawyer. He assists in disputes and mediates between people when they are unable to resolve their differences independently, making sure that decisions are fair according to his divine laws.

He appears as an intermediary for those who cannot come up with compromises themselves, ensuring fairness by following what he believes should be done according to his holy code of ethics.

ULLER

Uller is Thor's stepson—Sif's son from a previous marriage. Uller was born into extreme poverty while his father was away on an Earth expedition. His name means "bright one" or "glory," and he is associated with the Aurora Borealis in Scandinavia and other events that happen at night.

He has always felt inferior because Odin favors him over others. This feeling may be due to Odin being so powerful himself. Still, he often chooses people less capable than those available for tasks that someone stronger-minded can only accomplish. He lives in Ydalir, which translates to "Yew-dales."

He is a winter god that walks around on snowshoes. He used a bow and arrow as his weapon, and he was an excellent archer, skier, and hunter.

Uller is the Norse god of warriors, hunting, and single combat and was invoked when a lone warrior needed help. Some sources say Uller governed Asgard while Odin was away.

BRAGI

Bragi is the son of Odin and Gunlod, a giantess who had three nights of pleasure with him. He shares all of his poetry knowledge with others to enrich their lives by adding beauty where there was once only dullness.

More than just your average god, he's also a poet! And not just any type - Bragi writes poems that are so beautiful; they make people wiser.

In northern society, poets were important because they had the power to weave other people's fates with their words. They also passed judgment and prophecies, which gave them a higher status in that world than any other group of individuals. The tribe's poets were tasked with preserving the culture and history of their people through songs, stories, and poetry. They make sure that, no matter what happens to the tribe, they will not be forgotten by future generations.

Imagine a man who has the power to tell an infinite story from sunrise till sunset. Bragi, the Poet of Runes, is invoked for inspiration, and he's been described like Santa Claus or Father Time, with all-seeing eyes.

Bragi was quite famous among the Norse gods for having extraordinary powers and great luck, which made him one of their most important deities. He had a vast knowledge of runes and frequently wrote on them, giving people magical words to recite when casting spells. This allowed many poets over time to call upon him when they were seeking any kind of creative inspiration.

HOENIR

Hoenir raised sentient beings, taking them from a mindless existence. He is one of the few survivors to come out of Ragnarok, and he rejoices with his brother, Odin, when they finally meet again.

He was transported to the Vanir as a hostage to bring peace between the two tribes. He is revered among modern heathens for his prophecies and visions, which he would have while under their spell.

He is a god who has been revered for centuries by modern heathens, but it was not always that way. His name means "the silent one," and he became the hostage between the two tribes of gods to bring peace to both sides after years of conflict had raged on, with no end in sight. It wasn't until his wisdom began to be revealed through various prophesies and visions that people started turning their attention back towards him, realizing how important this deity was.

A lesser-known Aesir god who has been forgotten for centuries, he remained in the shadows while beings like Thor and Odin were worshiped by all of humanity.

The mentions of Hoenir in Old Norse literature are muddled and conflicting due to how little we know about him. Yet, it seems that his appearances had always counted when major events or decisive moments occurred.

He is mentioned in the Voluspa, a poem in the Poetic Edda, as having aided in creating the first humans, Ask and Embla. He appears there as part of a trio with Odin and Lodurr, a god about whom we know as little as we do about Hoenir.

After Ragnarok has gone, another verse from the Voluspa describes Hoenir practicing divination for the resurrected gods. Voluspa describes Hoenir performing this practice for those resurrected following their deaths during Ragnarok and proves it by bringing back Idunn, the goddess of youthfulness.

Hoenir is referenced in passing as Odin and Loki's journey companion in other legends too.

The Ynglinga Saga, written by the notoriously untrustworthy Snorri Sturluson, has one of the most known mentions of Hoenir in Old Norse literature. The Aesir and Vanir deities traded hostages in his rendition of "The War Between Gods."

Hoenir was born with a terrible curse. His beauty blinded his enemies, and without Mimir's assistance, he would have been unable to make any decisions. The Vanir were so taken by Hoenir's good looks that they appointed him as their chieftain but sadly found out how dim-witted Hoenir was when the time for battle against the Aesir came.

Mimir's words were wise, but they proved to be a fatal mistake for both him and his people. When Mimir advised others not to decide on anything while Hoenir was away, the Vanir believed this hesitation meant that the Aesir had cheated them out of their hostage swap. Consequently, when they discovered what had happened, the Vanir cut off Mimir's head and sent it back to the Aesir.

This picture of Hoenir as a bumbling, fearful fool is incompatible with his depictions in the remainder of Old Norse literature.

These different depictions don't paint a very coherent picture of Hoenir. If we ignore Snorri's portrayal, the picture becomes less muddled but still unclear. He is strongly connected to Odin and held many of Odin's attributes and skills, which seems reasonable to assume. The potential connection between the two is quite controversial among scholars, as there are no concrete indications to support this. However, it may be worth noting that Hoenir and other minor Norse gods were theoretically independent extensions of Odin in what many consider a poetic tale.

Lodurr

Lodurr has been forgotten by many because of his obscure role as an animator for humans. Little is known about Lodurr, but we know that he gives life to souls when they reach the underworld and then assigns them to one of three realms: Asgard (where warriors dwell), Midgard (the human realm), or Helheim.

It is unclear who Lodurr was, but he has been linked to Loki and the other Norse gods. Scholars have proposed that they may all be related in some way or just distant relatives.

Hermod

Hermod was the messenger of the gods. His role was to bring the words of their messages quickly and fearlessly. This importance can be seen in the account of Baldr's death, despite him being mentioned just once or twice throughout the mythology.

This elevates him above gods such as his half-brother Thor, the god of thunder; his brother Tyr, the one-handed god of war; and his younger brother Vidar, the silent god. Some scholars even consider Hermod to be Freya's husband, making him a great and fortunate god.

It is when Baldr dies that Hermod takes the centerstage.

The gods all cried for Baldr and wished him to return. Odin responded by allowing Hermod to ride Sleipnir, traveling over land, sea, or air. They could reach Hel's dark gate in this manner, allowing him to free Baldr from her clutches before he died a second time, in true death.

Hermod, who was already quick on his feet, added to the steed's pace, and the horse and rider rode to Helheim, the domain of Hel, the goddess of death and misery. It wasn't a realm where the living returned, so riding in there required quite a brass set, a treasure of the gods or not.

Hel asked a ransom since Hermod had come into her territory to beg for Baldr's freedom. Hel will only allow Baldr back into the real world if every living being on Earth sheds a tear for him. Not only that, but she also tasked Hermod with returning this message to Asgard.

Hermod is not referenced in any other notable tales, unlike Thor's wife, Sif, and his sons, Modi and Magni, who Thor eclipsed in their youth. However, his bravery and importance reveal that he was highly regarded and shined alongside the great and mighty gods. It's not always about how often your name appears on paper; it's sometimes about whatever story your name appears in that indicates how significant you are.

FRIGGA

Frigga is one of the most important goddesses in Norse mythology, but she's also largely unknown. She was married to Odin and was known for her cunning ways. Frigga has a lot on her plate: giving birth to all children everywhere, rewarding good mothers with riches like gold and silver while punishing bad mothers by sending them famine or disease, watching over pregnant women during childbirth so they have an easy delivery, and feeding newborns on golden plates when they are still too small to eat solid food themselves.

As Odin's wife, she was the formidable queen of Asgard, sitting beside her husband on his throne, but she ruled with him as a partner in all other aspects. The goddess had many different roles: love, beauty, fate, and procreation were just some of them, and each one revealed its secrets over time. She has authority over all realms.

Odin often overshadows Frigga. Still, she has a powerful status among the Norse gods, and it's nearly impossible to find any mention of her in surviving sources. Having descended from both the Vanir and Aesir tribes, her features appear to be an amalgamation of Freya (goddess of the Vanir tribes) with elements from both tribes, which shows a mutual evolution of their alliance over time.

Frigga is a goddess who has knowledge of everything but does not speak it. She resides in the sacred hall of Fensalir with twelve handmaids, assisting her during worship and rituals to make sure that she knows what's going on outside. As well as being important for childbirth, pregnancy, and children, Frigga also oversees marriages, which are considered extremely powerful unions between two families because they tie them together through generations of descendants forever.

Fulla

Fulla is Frigga's sister, most faithful handmaiden, and chief companion. Her given name means "plenty." She is considered the keeper of Frigga's treasure box, which plays a crucial role in any lady's home. As Frigga's loyal advisor, Fulla knows all of her secrets and works with her on all of her schemes.

Saga

Her name is derived from Old Norse and means "to speak" or "to inform." She is an Aesir historian, a collector of family tales, a poet, and a skald. She lives in a large hall called Sokkvabekk and is Odin's frequent drinking partner. Librarians, historians, and researchers worship her as a goddess. She prayed for inspiration while writing, organizing her life, and researching her ancestors.

EIR

Due to her healing skills, she is only referenced twice in the Eddas. She is known as the "greatest physician" since she heals all women who seek her out. Herbs, surgical procedures, religious and magical spells, runes, and even a sort of acupuncture were all part of the heathen culture's healing arsenal. She's empathetic but objective, like the doctor you've been looking for but can't seem to find. She relaxes you by calming, centering, and grounding you.

Modern Asatruars frequently worship her for good health, relief from illness, or assistance if someone they care about becomes ill. People all over the world follow Eir's example by seeking her comfort during times when their loved ones need it most, as well as assistance in staying healthy themselves. Eir was often called on to help the Norse healers called "skalder," experts in reading omens and predicting diseases. Eir's name comes from the Old Norse word for "help" or "mercy."

GEFION

Her given name means "the giving one." She is well remembered for how she defeated Sweden's King Gylfi to win the island of Zealand. She approached him as a beggar woman, and in exchange for some amusement, he promised her all the land she could cultivate in a day and a night. She moved to Jotunheim, married a giant, and had four sons before turning them into oxen. She returned to Gylfi's land and plowed it so thoroughly and quickly that the island of Zealand was severed from the mainland. Gefion and her plow are even shown in a fountain in

Copenhagen. She is commonly referred to as the goddess of material fortune by modern heathens, who seek her assistance in financial matters. In the Lokasenna, Odin chastises Loki for bothering her, noting that Gefion knows men's destiny as well as Odin does.

Gna

Her name is derived from the old Norse word gnaefa, which means "to tower" or "to rise high." She is Frigga's messenger, running errands for her mistress across the nine planets. She is tasked with finding a quick solution to her problems.

Syntax

Frigga's hall, Fensalir, has a gatekeeper named Sin. Her name means "denial" or "refusal." She acts like a bouncer at a bar, barring the doors to anyone who might cause a commotion. Syn is the god of impulse and passion, the one who stirs up trouble.

Hlin

Her given name translates to "protector." She is tasked with ensuring the safety of all Frigga's mortals. It is stated in Voluspa that

Another woe awaited Hlin,
When he goes to Odin to fight the wolf,
And the slayer of Beli fights a battle with Surt:
Then Frigg's husband will fall lifeless.

Many heathens read this to suggest that Hlin will give Frigga the strength to carry on after her husband's death. She was summoned by wives who had lost their husbands in combat and required her strength to carry on.

SJOFN

Her name is derived from an Old Norse word that means "affection." She opens people's hearts to love and the kinds of relationships that feed our souls. Sjofn is the goddess of romantic love.

She is a guardian of marriage and sexual fidelity who punishes adulterers with blindness or sickness and blesses faithful partners with fertility. Married couples call on her to help them conceive children even when they have difficulty doing so. Pregnant women often invoked Sjofn for protection against the pain that accompanied giving birth.

LOFN

"Comforter" is the meaning of her name. During the ups and downs of a relationship, she offers support and hope. She even went out of her way to beg Odin and Frigga for permission to marry a couple, and the word "permission" comes from her name. Lofn is the goddess of love, and she is passionate about relationships.

PREV

Her name isn't mentioned much in the lore, but she was extremely wise and never overlooked anything. When you need to view a problem more clearly, work with her. Vor is a goddess of perception, and she can help you see what's going on.

Vor never gets into disputes with other deities because her job is to keep an eye out for troublemakers, so they do not have a chance to cause problems.

Var

She is claimed to have presided over all holy oaths, particularly marriage vows, as her name means "vow" or "pledge." It is also her responsibility to hold those who violate vows accountable.

Snotra

Her reputation for being bright and smart is known about her (which is the meaning of her name). She is renowned as the Aesir's diplomat, a goddess of etiquette and correct behavior.

Sif

Norse mythology has many tales from the ancient past, but few about the fertility goddess, Sif. Despite her absence from their scriptures, Asatruars regard her as a symbol of crops and golden hair.

Sif is frequently worshiped for her dominion over field crops. Her golden hair has become a symbol for modern Asatruars, who see it as representing ripe harvests in the fields.

The theory is based on a narrative in Snorri's Edda in which Loki rips off Sif's golden hair. Scholars in the late 1800s regarded the narrative as a metaphor for the fertility of the field's crops.

Sif is a divine symbol that city-dwelling Asatruar can also connect. Thor's thunderstorms bring her crops to life with his abundant summer showers, which causes her to grow further in power during these seasons.

Nanna

Nanna is a mystery, save for the fact that she is married to Baldur and her name means "the courageous one." She joins him in Hel's realm after his death when she dies of sadness. She and Baldr return to Asgard after Ragnarok.

Idun

Idun is a youthful goddess who gifts the world with eternal youth. Her work has been replicated by artists and poets, but it's her job to ensure that our lives are never-ending cycles of birth, death, and rebirth in accordance with the year's cycle from spring to winter - which encompasses much more than just twelve months: each one marks an important stage in life's journey.

Idun was vital for every rite involving human sacrifice because she ensured everyone would live again. When you think of Idun, the first thing that comes to mind is her eternal youth. Her juices are what give all living things, including humans, life, and hope. If she were not around, then we would have no seasons or a universe at all!

Idun's special power preserved the juice from fruit, so it never spoils. This also made her responsible for giving new earthly fruits their seeds to keep the Earth alive with fresh food sources.

Nerthus

Tacitus only mentions her in Germania, where he compares her to Terra Mater. She was not only attractive and lifegiving through the richness she provided to humanity, but she was also destructive through storms, earthquakes, volcanoes, and other natural disasters.

Sigyn

She is only referenced three times in the legend, and they all refer to the same event: she is Loki's wife, and she faithfully stays by his side when he is bound, holding the bowl over him to catch the poison pouring from the snake overhead. Many heathens consider her to be an abusive spouse or a faithful wife. The majority of what we know about this deity is pure UPG.

Hel

Hel was a Norse goddess who ruled over Helheim, the Norse underworld. She had pale skin, and she welcomed anybody that came to her domain with open arms. Her name itself has many hidden connotations: "hel" means "concealment," whereas, in Old English, it meant both "to cover" or "a covered place."

Loki, a god who was constantly stirring up trouble for the other gods on Earth, and Angrboda (a giantess) had one daughter they loved dearly, Hel. She is mean-spirited by nature, but her parents knew she would someday be useful to them with her powers of indifference. When they had a daughter, Loki wanted to name her "the one who brings joy," but his wife refused and said the child should be called Hel.

Loki felt very guilty because he was not able to protect his daughter from harm when she grew up, so, instead of punishing her for causing trouble on Earth, as some gods would have done, he preferred to punish her by sending her to a dark place where she would rule and have power over those who had been cast out of Asgard.

The gods were not happy about this, but they agreed that it was Loki's right as a father.

When Baldr dies, Hel makes her most important appearance in Norse mythology. Hermod was dispatched to speak with the goddess about returning Baldr from death as all living things already mourned him. The goddess of death refused and said that she would not give up his life so easily, which led them into a battle where Hel killed Hermod but received wounds herself during their fight.

Hel had a condition for his return. If every single element shed a tear for Baldr, then she would release him from the underworld to live again among humans on Earth. Hermod was determined that nothing and none should be spared, so he made sure everything cried out for his brother's life, except one giantess with no tongue. Therefore, Balder remained in the underworld.

Vanir

The Vanir were the "Paleolithic" pantheon of gods, who were eventually taken over and overshadowed by the Aesir. They are connected with fertility and growth.

The War of the Aesir versus the Vanir—Gullvieg, the Vanir goddess, came to reside with the Aesir. She adored gold, just like the other Vanir goddesses, and it was all she could think. Asgard suffered greatly as a result of her bad views, so no one was happy. Gullvieg was tied up, wounded three times with a spear, and burned three times by Odin. The Vanir demanded reparations for her torture, as well as recognition on par with the Aesir. When the Aesir refused, the war started. It was finally settled with a ritual involving the gods spitting into a bowl, resulting in the creation of Kvasir (a creature who toured the Earth teaching his knowledge and was subsequently killed by two dwarves who made his blood into mead). This is known as Odrir or the mead of poetry. Vanir Njordr, Freya, and Frey, led by Kvasir, went to dwell with the Aesir, while Hoenir and Mimir went to dwell with the Vanir. Hoenir and Mimir were both wise, but the Vanir felt duped because Hoenir was slow to speak. They accused Mimir of covertly giving Hoenir counsel. Mimir was beheaded and taken to Asgard, where Odin stored and used it to obtain insight.

FREYA

Freya was known as a passionate and sensual Norse goddess who shared attributes with Frigga. Freya, the famous volva of their era, possessed powers similar to those of her counterpart in Aesir: they used sacred magic to determine fates and bring about beneficial changes within the systems. They did this by transforming into falcons using feathers from birds sacred to them both - the golden eagle for Freya or the white-tailed seagull for Frigga - and soaring out over the Earth to see if anything had happened, then returning home to tell Odin before making any decisions on whether it should be allowed or not.

Freya is a witch with the power of weaving. She is a sorceress that can create new worlds out of thin air, breathe life into memories and dreams alike until they're real in her palm. Freya has always had an interest in magic. For example, one day, she experimented with some runes when suddenly, something incredible happened; one rune started glowing brighter than all the others before fading away into nothingness.

Women in Viking society were considered powerful, wise, and respected. The volva was a sorceress who would travel from village to village performing her magic arts for food, clothes, or lodging as payment when needed. According to Norse legend, they were regarded with awe and terror by the people because of their power over life and death.

FREYR

In ancient Scandinavian lore, Freyr is a deity that prefers the company of beautiful women. He was revered and adored by his followers, who were overjoyed to know that he had specifically blessed them with prosperity in their lives. In addition to this powerful gift, it became known that Freyr was also responsible for producing rain and sunshine on Earth, which made him an important figure not only as a god but as a ruler too. This deity favored all things masculine, such as strength or power, whereas, for females, it represented beauty and fertility. These two ideas combined gave us one of our first images depicting nature's balance between male/female energy, where we see how each complements the other perfectly.

The god Freyr is revered as the "foremost of the gods." Because of his capacity to bestow wealth and prosperity on those who made him happy, no one despised him.

While some associate Freyr with fertility, he is also often depicted as a protector of the environment. Whether in need of food or clean water, people would come to him for help and guidance, which led them into cleaner waters.

Freyr has had many roles throughout history, but one thing remains consistent: his association with nature's beauty and prosperity. From protecting from illnesses like cancer to ensuring bountiful harvests that feed communities across Europe each year, Freyr was always there when needed most by those who worshiped him faithfully.

NJORDR

Njordr, the Vanir god of the sea, lives atop Noatun, a cliff overlooking the water. Skadi, Thiassi's daughter, is his wife. He is the patron saint of sailors and fishermen, who pray to him for calm seas and plentiful harvests. He is still revered by heathens today for his serene composure and ability to navigate, whether on a map or in the corporate world.

Jotnar

The plural of jotunn, a Norse word denoting a divine entity different from Norse gods and goddesses, is jotnar. Jotnar is known by many different names and words, including theur, risi, and troll. Giant is frequently used as a synonym for jotunn. Jotnar, on the other hand, is not always massive in size and appearance. Jotnar can be frighteningly hideous or breathtakingly lovely. Odin is a descendent of the jotnar, and other Norse gods, like Geror and Skadi, have also been described as jotnar.

They are members of a race of natural spirits with superhuman powers, said to oppose the Aesir and Vanir races, but they frequently mix with or marry them. Their otherworldly home is Jötunheimr, one of Norse cosmology's nine planets separated from Midgard, the human realm, by steep mountains or deep forests.

In later Scandinavian folklore, the nature spirit troll (derived from the word "magic") assumes many of the functions of the older idea of jotunn.

The jotnar were the first race to appear when the universe was created. Like the Aesir, a jotunn appears in almost every story or poem. They are the primary villains in most lore, but they are also the wives, parents, grandparents, and friends of the Aesir and Vanir gods.

Ý I was the first in this great race, which arose from the Ginnungagap River. "Just as coldness and all things grim sprang from Niflheimr, so what was faced close to Muspelheim was hot and bright, while Ginnungagap was as gentle as a windless sky," Snorri writes in Gylfaginning. And when the rime and the warm wind met, it froze and dripped, and there was a quickening from these flowing drops due to the power of the heat's source, and it took the shape of a man, and he was named Mir.

Ýmir's children had many offspring of their own, and they intermarried with Búri, the first of the gods to appear, whose son married a jotunn called Bestla. After a few years, there appears to have been a lot of enmity and conflict between the races, and Ýmir was eventually killed by Bestla's sons, Odin, Vili, and Vé.

Out of the enormous body of the fallen jotunn, the brothers created the Midgard. His blood created the oceans, rivers, and lakes, and the dome of his skull became the sky stretching over the Earth. Ýmir's brain, hair, and bones became clouds, trees, mountains, and hills, respectively. The race of dwarfs also appears at this point in the story, emerging into a more human-like form from the giant's flesh as small worms or maggots.

The gods created a type of barrier out of Ýmir's eyelashes, separating the giants' land of Jötunheimr from the realm of humankind. It was then the gods' responsibility to keep an eye on this border and protect their new creations from the jotnars' destructive elemental energies.

The distinctions between giants and gods are sometimes stark and spectacular, and other times they are imperceptible. With claws, teeth, and malformed faces or bodies, some of the jotnar are horrible or dreadful in appearance. They can be huge or average-sized humans. Some of them have several heads, such as Þrívaldi, who had nine, and others, such as Jormungandr, Sleipnir, and Fenrir, are not humanoid at all. The gods' and giants' relationship has always been complicated.

Skadi

Skadi is the main and most well-known jotunn. She is a tough mountain warrior and very friendly to all those who enjoy the deep woods and high peaks. She's known as the guardian of forests, mountains, and hunting grounds and the ruler of clan members living in her territory. Skadi lives up to her title of "protector" by being fiercely protective of what she loves, just as much as any mother would be with her children.

Skadi is a powerful goddess known for her mastery of the mountains and forests. She's often found hunting in these places with wolves at her side—she loves to spend time exploring their depths. Skadi prefers spending most of her days on top of really high mountain peaks where it's so cold that even mortals will freeze if they stay there too long without shelter or supplies.

Chapter 5: The Concepts Of Wyrd And Orlog

The concepts of Wyrd and Orlog are probably the most perplexing in the Norse value system. Is Orlog like clay, which we shape into our Wyrd? Or is it more like Karma? Maybe a combination of the two? Is there clay-like Karma?

The ancient Scandinavians looked to the past for guidance, believing the future to be predetermined but unknown. For example, the three Norns, who later became the three witches of Shakespeare's *Macbeth*, foretold everyone's fate at birth.

In Norse mythology, Wyrd and Orlog are linked to the concepts of time and causality. The Tree of Life, Yggdrasil, and the three Norns are all related to Wyrd and Orlog. The connections are explored in the sections that follow.

We know the following from the Voluspa:

I know an ash tree, named Yggdrasil:
Sparkling showers are shed on its leaves
That drip dew, into the dales below,
By Urda's well it waves evergreen,
Stands over that still pool,
Near it a bower whence now there come
The Fate Maidens, first Urda,
Skulda second, scorer of runes,
Then Verdandi, third of the Norns:
The laws that determine the lives of men
They fixed forever and their fate sealed.

Urda, Verdandi, and Skulda - what was, is, and shall be - are the three Norns. Next to Yggdrasil is a well named after Urda, implying that the past is the essential factor. The three Norns arrive at each child's birth and pronounce their doom, their fate. Orlog is the Norns' name for destiny, and they control, decree, and pronounce it. Thus, your fate is sealed from the moment you are born.

Urda, Verdandi, and Skulda sat beside the well in the hollow of Yggdrasil's great root. Urda was old and had white hair, and Verdandi was lovely, but Skulda could hardly be seen because she sat far back, and her hair fell over her face and eyes. Urda, Verdandi, and Skulda knew everything there was to know about the past, the present, and the future. When Odin looked at them, he saw right into Skulda's eyes. So long, long did he stand with God-like eyes on the Norns while the others listened to the swans' murmurs and the leaves of Yggdrasil falling into Urda's well.

The past is ancient, the present is lovely, but the future is difficult to predict. The Norns are the ones who weave the web of deeds. Layer upon layer, events are stacked on top of one another, each thread fulfilling its role to create more extensive and more beautiful patterns. Urda and Wyrd are linked in some way. Both have the same meaning. The German verb *werden* is related to the concept of Wyrd. It's used in the present tense. That is what will happen. There is a sense of impending doom. The process by which our past actions shape our present is known as Wyrd. Actions have ramifications. Orlog is what has to happen - fate - the laws that force things to happen the way they do.

Ragnarok is mythical in Norse Paganism.

Ragnarok is the epic battle between the gods and the giants. They are aware that they will have to fight, that the fight will occur, and that the fight will have an inevitable outcome. The gods have the power to reveal your fate.

Let's compare the deterministic and probabilistic perspectives. Your fate is determined at birth, according to Norse mythology. In contrast, we prefer to think of each action as having a chance of succeeding. Everything is possible; each of the six dice numbers has an equal opportunity of being thrown. However, we only roll one digit at a time, and since we can't go back in time to re-throw the dice, no other outcome is possible at that time. Probability expresses our apprehension about the future. However, once it occurs, it is recorded. There is no other option. This is what Wyrd is all about.

Orlog is the act of laying down, transforming uncertainty, turning the open-endedness of the future into the past. As Albert Einstein famously stated, "God does not play dice." Every action is pre-planned. We don't know how because far too many variables determine each outcome. Wyrd and Orlog share this viewpoint. The past impacts the present, and the present affects the future. The gods meet at the well of Urda to discuss probability, which is our uncertainty about the future. They are aware of men's fate and destiny. The number we rolled on the dice was the only number we could have moved at the time. Therefore, we cannot know ahead of time. We can express our level of uncertainty by saying, for example, that we have a one in six chance of rolling a five.

This is correct; if a hundred people roll a dice six times, we should expect a hundred fives. However, no other outcome was possible for each other than the one rolled at that particular moment in time. Therefore, we must accept our fate with dignity and honor, as it results from our actions. We participated in the game and rolled the dice, so we either win or lose.

Yggdrasil is a mythical creature from the Norse mythology.

The leaves of the Yggdrasil tree fall into Urda's well. The leaves have fallen and remain in the well, layer upon layer, with newer ones on top, and the older ones only visible after the more recent layers have been removed. Our past actions shape our present. We've taken a chance and will live with the results.

Let's say a woman goes to the doctor, she's married, and she's having trouble getting pregnant. The doctor prescribes a medication, claiming that 60% of women who take it become pregnant within a year. She accepts it because she wishes to start a family. According to the doctor, she has a 60% chance of becoming pregnant. However, the woman is either pregnant or not. She can't possibly be 60% pregnant.

From his perspective, the doctor is correct. After a year, six out of ten of the women he gave the pill to became pregnant. So the outcome is wholly predetermined for each woman. I'm not sure if she's pregnant or not. We could predict whether she would become pregnant after taking the medication if we knew all of the variables involved and could compute them. Otherwise, the gods will make the final decision.

The Ideal Computer

Consider the following scenario: A perfect computer has been created to calculate all actions and outcomes. It is so quick that it calculates everything in real-time. However, the computer would also have to consider its existence and predictions, as they impact the future. A feedback loop would allow the computer to feed its results back into the computation. If actions and consequences are unpredictable, if each computer cycle produces a different result, the process will veer off and never finish. On the other hand, if the computer computes a better answer every cycle, the results will eventually converge.

We assume the computer completes the task in a finite number of cycles and returns a result immediately. All actions are predetermined in this case, and everything that occurs must occur. This is the same idea as Einstein's that God does not play dice, as well as the Norns deciding each man's fate and the gods meeting at the well of Urda for council. If such a computer existed and could predict every action's outcomes, we would lose faith in the gods because we would know what would happen next.

We have become gods in our own right, equal to Odin. Assuming that there is order in the world and that it does not devolve into chaos, all actions are predetermined, and the Norns have predicted our fate. Ragnarok represents the battle of order versus chaos, gods versus giants, where once there was order, chaos triumphed, and order was restored out of chaos. The perfect computer confirms our suspicions. Either everything is predetermined, or everything is chaotic.

Chapter 6: Get To Know The Asatru And Norse Symbols

Yggdrasil

This is an image of Yggdrasil, the Norse World Ash, a representation of the fabled tree that connects the nine worlds or planes of existence. This artwork may be seen on the famed Överhogdal Tapestries, which date from 1066 and represent the events of Ragnarok, a pre-Christian Norse apocalyptic prophecy. The serpent Jormungandr guards the World Ash. Yggdrasil is one of several names for the Cosmic Axis, also known as the Universal World Tree, found in all human cultures.

The serpent or Dragon Nidhogg lurking at the tree's base, the Rooster Gullinkambi (golden comb) dwelling at the tree's apex, and the squirrel Ratatosk carrying messages between them are just a few of the creatures who call Yggdrasil home. These animals can be considered human body analogies. Yggdrasil is where Odin was hung upside down for nine nights to receive the Rune Alphabet, according to Norse tradition. Underneath the World Ash's roots is Mimir, the spring to which Odin gave an eye in exchange for wisdom.

The Horn of Odin (Triple horn, Horned triskele)

Odin's Triple Horn is a stylized representation of the Norse God. Three intertwined drinking horns make up this emblem, often worn or shown as a sign of devotion to the contemporary Asatru faith. The horns appear in Odin's mythology and are remembered in ancient Norse toasting rites. The majority of the stories revolve around the deity's search for Odhroerir, a magical mead made from the blood of the wise god Kvasir.

According to legend, Odin uses his brains and skills to procure the brew over three days; the three horns represent the three draughts of the mystical mead.

Valknut

The valknut was one of the most popular but puzzling symbols employed by the Vikings. It is associated with death and burials across the Viking culture, yet it is not mentioned in any remaining literary sources. This implies we'll have to guess its significance based on what we know about Vikings in general.

So, what does the valknut sign most likely mean?

Three overlapping triangles make up the valknut symbol. It existed in two forms in the Viking world. Three overlapping but independent triangles represent the Borromean shape, whereas a single line represents the unicursal shape. These are thought to be variants of the same symbol because they exist in the same archeological context.

Valknut is a modern Norwegian moniker given to the sign, not a traditional Viking name. It combines the terms "valr" for slain warriors and "knut" for knot to obtain the "knot of killed warriors." Valknut seems connected with the dead and Odin; hence, this name was chosen.

The origin of the valknut has been the subject of several speculations. Some historians believe it was a sign of rebirth, while others believe it was a protective shield for the dead soul. The nine points of the triangle have often been linked to Norse mythology's nine worlds, while the three interwoven triangles represent the connection between Earth, Heaven, and Hell. Odin was a master of euphoric Seidr magic, and the emblem has been linked to him.

Valknut was also linked to Valhalla, the warrior afterlife in which all Vikings hoped to be reunited. This is supported by the fact that death is associated with Odin. It is also believed that this was a symbol that identified the dead as residents of Valhalla. However, it could have been a magical emblem utilized in Seidr magic for this purpose.

Vegvisir

A Viking rune stave, or runic compass, is a mystical item intended to aid in sea navigation. According to tradition, this apotropaic (protective) emblem was allegedly carved into seagoing vessels to ensure their safe return. The most frequent portrayal of the rune originates from the Galdrabók, an Icelandic grimoire from the 17th century.

It is most popularly associated with the aegishjalmer, utilized by Asatru adherents to signify spiritual direction and identification. Bjork, the Icelandic pop singer, has the most known example of a tattoo.

The Nine Worlds

This is a visual representation of the nine worlds, which are separated into three regions in Norse cosmology. In the Upper Realm, the Aesir's home, Asgard, is governed by Odin, the Norse god's ruler. Vanaheim is where the Vanir call home. Freyr is the ruler of Alfheim, the realm of elves.

The rainbow bridge, below, is connected to the upper world by Bifrost.

Midgard, which means "middle earth," is the physical plane's home for humans. Midgard is encircled by the ocean, which is home to Jormungandr, the world's first snake. The abode of the jotnar, or giants, is Jotunheim. Svartalfheim is an underground kingdom inhabited by evil elves.

The Kingdom of the Dead, the lowest level, likewise has three realms.

Niflheim is a frigid wasteland ruled by the goddess Hel, with endless darkness. The land of the fire giants is Muspelheim. Hel is the place where the dead goes to rest.

HELM OF AWE (AEGISHJALMUR)

The Helm of Awe is one of Norse mythology's most enigmatic and powerful symbols. Without knowing what it represents, just looking at its design inspires awe and fear: eight spiked trident-like arms spread out from a central point as if guarding that center by going on the attack against any hostile forces surrounding it.

This magical symbol appeared to be designed to produce such overwhelming power. The havoc-wreaking dragon Fafnir credits his apparent immortality using the Helm of Awe in the Fáfnismál in the Poetic Edda.

JORMUNGANDR

Jormungandr, also known as Iormungand or Jormung, is the serpentine son of Loki, the mischievous god, and Angrboda, the frost goddess. He is a monster serpent doomed to die in the Battle of Ragnarok at Thor's hands. In an attempt to prevent the inevitable, Odin seized the huge serpent and tossed him into the sea, where he grew so huge that he ringed the earth, according to tradition.

The Midgard Serpent is another name for him. Jormungandr is sometimes depicted as having three heads, indicating that he exists in all three realms of Norse Cosmology.

THOR'S HAMMER (MJOLNIR)

Mjolnir, or Thor's Hammer, is an antique Norse emblem, a stylized portrayal of Thor's fabled magical weapon. Mjolnir, which translates as "lightning," represents the god's command of thunder and lightning. After being thrown, the Hammer Mjolnir was famous to always return.

Believers wore the Thor's Hammer amulet frequently as a symbol of protection, a practice that persisted long after the majority of the Norse people had converted to Christianity. It is frequently used as a sign of Norse heritage and as a symbol of Asatru faith adherents.

The Wolf's Cross, or Dragon's Cross, is a later version of the Mjolnir associated with early Norse Christianity.

RUNES (RUNIC ALPHABET)

Runes are a Norse alphabet made up of characters used for mystical purposes developed around 200 BCE. The alphabet was discovered in a vision by Odin while he was hung upside down and injured for nine days on Yggdrasil, according to Norse mythology.

The word 'rune' literally means 'secret' or 'whisper.' Elder Futhark is the oldest. It comprises three sets of eight letters; there have been as many as thirty-three runic characters and as few as sixteen at different points throughout history. Runes have long been employed as a divinatory tool, and some researchers believe that there was once a separate class of diviners who specialized in rune reading.

Runes are currently being made and used by Asatru believers as a meditation and divination tool. It is customary for people to make their own set of rune stones.

Celtic Shield Knot

The Celtic shield knot comes in a variety of styles, including modern stylized forms. The shield knot's four distinct corners are its distinguishing feature. This symbol is typically just a looped square with a circle in the center, but it can also encircle.

Like all Celtic knots, this knot has no beginning or end and comprises a single thread that weaves and interlaces with itself. The design has no loose ends, giving it a seamless, never-ending appearance.

The Celtic shield knot was utilized as a symbol of protection to ward off evil spirits and danger. Many troops will bring amulets and charms with them when they travel to war. This emblem was used on the battlefield to shield warriors from damage.

On the other hand, the shield knot can symbolize eternal love, unity, and loyalty among friends, family, and lovers. Its never-ending loop, with no beginning or end, symbolizes everlasting love, while the knot picture symbolizes an unbreakable relationship. Today, the connotation of love is the more prominent one.

Troll Cross

Ancient Scandinavians thought that iron crosses protect trolls, elves, and other dark creatures. The trollkors is a symbol based on this idea.

The trollkors, or troll cross, has been used by Scandinavians for a long time, although no real archeological evidence has been discovered.

Despite being widely acknowledged as part of Swedish tradition, the first troll cross to be recorded was jewelry created by Kari Erlands of Sweden in the 1990s after discovering the symbol in her grandparents' barn.

Kari Erlands claimed to have reproduced the stated protective rune, but the piece does resemble the Odal or Othala in the Elder Futhark; therefore, her claim is unsubstantiated.

The estate, history, possession, and inheritance are all represented by the symbol.

This symbol was extensively used to represent the house, family, and everything linked with it before the twentieth century. The emblem was commonly seen near where cows were kept in those days because people believed it safeguarded the animals from trolls.

The troll cross has a striking resemblance to a prominent Nazi symbol during World War II. The use of this symbol by neo-Nazi organizations and many others not linked with the neo-Nazis persisted after the war.

THE SOLAR CROSS

The solar cross is the world's oldest religious emblem, appearing in religious art since the dawn of time throughout Asia, America, Europe, and India. It represents the solar calendar marked by the solstices and is made out of an equal-armed cross within a circle. The equinoxes are sometimes marked as well, creating an eight-armed wheel. The swastika is also a type of solar cross.

In Northern Europe, the sun cross, in its simplest form (seen above), is known as Odin's cross, after the Norse pantheon's chief god. Asatruars frequently adopt it as an insignia. The term "cross" stems from the Old Norse word "kros."

HUGIN AND MUNIN

Hugin and Munin are two ravens who aid Odin's spirit in Norse mythology.

Odin and ravens have a long and complicated relationship. Visual images of Odin on helmets and jewelry date back to the sixth and seventh centuries AD, well before the Viking Age began in the late eighth century. They frequently depict him with one or more ravens.

Why did Odin have such a strong and long-lasting bond with ravens of all kinds? The answer is essentially related to Odin's function as a god of war and death, as those kennings suggest. Ravens, being carrion birds, were present during battles and were among the main beneficiaries.

GUNGNIR

Odin's powerful spear, Gungnir, is named for him.

Gungnir is the weapon most regularly and powerfully linked with Odin in the recorded Norse tales. Both poetry and visual art show that this bond is strong and long-lasting. It dates back to the ninth century, when Bragi Boddason, a poet, referred to Odin as Gungnir's shaker. Odin is frequently depicted with a spear in pre-Christian Scandinavian art. The spear is one of his most common iconographic features. Such portrayals may be found in Viking Age rune stones and Bronze Age rock carvings of a spear deity who could very well be Odin (although it's impossible to determine for sure due to the early date and absence of other identifying qualities).

Gungnir is no ordinary spear, as one might expect from a god's weapon. According to the legend of the gods' greatest treasures, it was crafted by the dwarves, the universe's most proficient smiths. Gungnir's point is reported to contain runes engraved into it, [5] which, through magic, augment its aim and deadliness. Archeology reveals that the Norse and other Germanic peoples carved runes into some of their spears, [6] presumably in imitation of Gungnir, the fabled model.

Other features of Gungnir were unquestionably legendary models for human behavior. This is especially true when it comes to the spear's function in Odin's human sacrifices.

Spirit Ship

The spirit ship frequently appears in Norse pictograph stone sculptures, dating back to the fifth millennium CE.

The spirit ship is most typically seen on burial monuments, where it depicts the afterlife trip. The sign is linked to the Viking tradition of transporting the dead to the afterlife atop a flaming ship.

Surprisingly, the ancient sculptures show a watercraft that looks exactly like a Viking longship. Similar engravings reaching back to 800 BCE have been discovered in Canada.

Sleipnir

Sleipnir (Norse for "gliding one") is Odin's mythical eight-legged horse. Odin is transported between the worlds of the gods and the realm of matter by Sleipnir. The eight legs represent the four cardinal directions and Sleipnir's ability to move both on land and in the air.

Sleipnir's eight legs were most likely symbolic of the solar wheel's eight spokes, and they were most likely related to an

76

older incarnation of Odin as a sun god. Sleipnir's ability to travel instantly associates him with sunshine, and there is even evidence that Odin himself was once anthropomorphized as a horse.

According to Norse mythology, Sleipnir is the son of the god Loki and Svaldifari, the giant's big horse. Sleipnir is similar to the Celtic gods' otherworldly horses, such as Manannan Mac Lir and Im Dagda.

Irminsul

The Asatru faith uses the irminsul as a symbol. The historical Norse irminsul was a solar phallic pillar used in early Anglo-Saxon religious worship and demolished by Charlemagne in 772 AD.

Its specific meaning is unknown, talhough it could be linked to the Anglo-Saxon deity Irmin, who may be related to the Norse God Tyr, as the shape of the rune letter tyr suggests. The World Tree Yggdrasil, a symbol of the axis Mundi (world axis), an emblem of man and the universe, was most likely tied to the irminsul.

The Web of Wyrd

The Web of Wyrd is a sign in Norse mythology that signifies the past, present, and future interconnection. It is one of the lesser-known Nordic emblems.

According to legend, the Norns/Nornir, the Shapers of Destiny in Norse mythology, knitted the Web of Wyrd.

The nine-stave symbol comprises all of the runes, indicating "possibilities" that the past, present, and future have brought and may bring.

Skulda was thought to be one of the Norns who wove the web; hence, it's also known as "Skulda's net."

Wyrd refers to the universe as a whole, a gigantic spider's web in which everything is linked and analogically interconnected, to the point where massive galaxies can mimic cell structures and the genome of living things. There is a macrocosm and a microcosm. While structural and functional analyses continue to captivate scientists, the old Norse and Germanic cultures would argue that time and purpose are important.

THE MISTRESS OF ANIMALS

As she's known, the Mistress of Animals is a fourth-century stone figure of an unidentified Norse goddess. She is frequently depicted holding serpents in each hand, referencing the ancient Babylonian Goddess Ishtar or the Cretan Bee Goddess. Because she is in a birthing posture, she is most likely a creatrix.

The goddess as the creatrix is most likely symbolized by the triskele above her head. It comprises three creatures representing the Celtic spheres of existence: the boar representing the earth, the serpent representing the sea, and the bird representing the sky.

NIDSTANG

Nidstang translates to "curse pole." The nidstang (also known as a "nithing" or "niding" pole) is a traditional Scandinavian way of formally cursing or hexing someone. A wooden pole or stake was built in a ceremony and inscribed with the desired outcome.

A horse's head or carcass was placed on the pole towards where the curse was intended to be sent. Today, the nidstang is more likely to be virtual, with a virtual horse's head accompanying it (I'm sure the animals are relieved).

Einherjar

The Einherjar are the heroic dead collected by the Valkyries from the battlefield and divided between Odin and the goddess Freya in Norse Pagan (Asatru) mythology. These warrior spirits reside in Valhalla with the Aesir, where they train for the last battle of Ragnarok, in which they will fight alongside Odin and the Aesir. The Einherjar are Neolithic relics frequently represented as armed servants of Odin in Norse burial objects.

Oseberg

This enigmatic figure is depicted as an ornament on a metal bucket found in the wreckage of a Viking ship discovered in Oseberg, Norway, around 800 CE. Because of his lotus-posture position and ornamental swastikas, this image is known as the Oseberg Buddha. He is most likely a portrayal of the Thor.

Julbock

In Scandinavian cultures, the julbock, or Yule-goat, is a common symbol of the winter holidays. The goat was the gods' mode of transport in the Norse pagan religion; early pictures of Odin on a goat-drawn cart are hauntingly similar to later representations of Santa Claus.

The Yule-goat gained popularity as a trickster character, a stand-in for the devil who followed the elf Tomten, later St Nick on gift-giving trips as Christianity became the norm. Men from the villages began dressing up as julbocks and playing pranks on the unsuspecting.

In modern times, the julbock is most commonly symbolized by a straw goat figurine, usually fashioned from the last grains of the harvest, packed into red ribbons, and kept as a symbol of hope for the New Year.

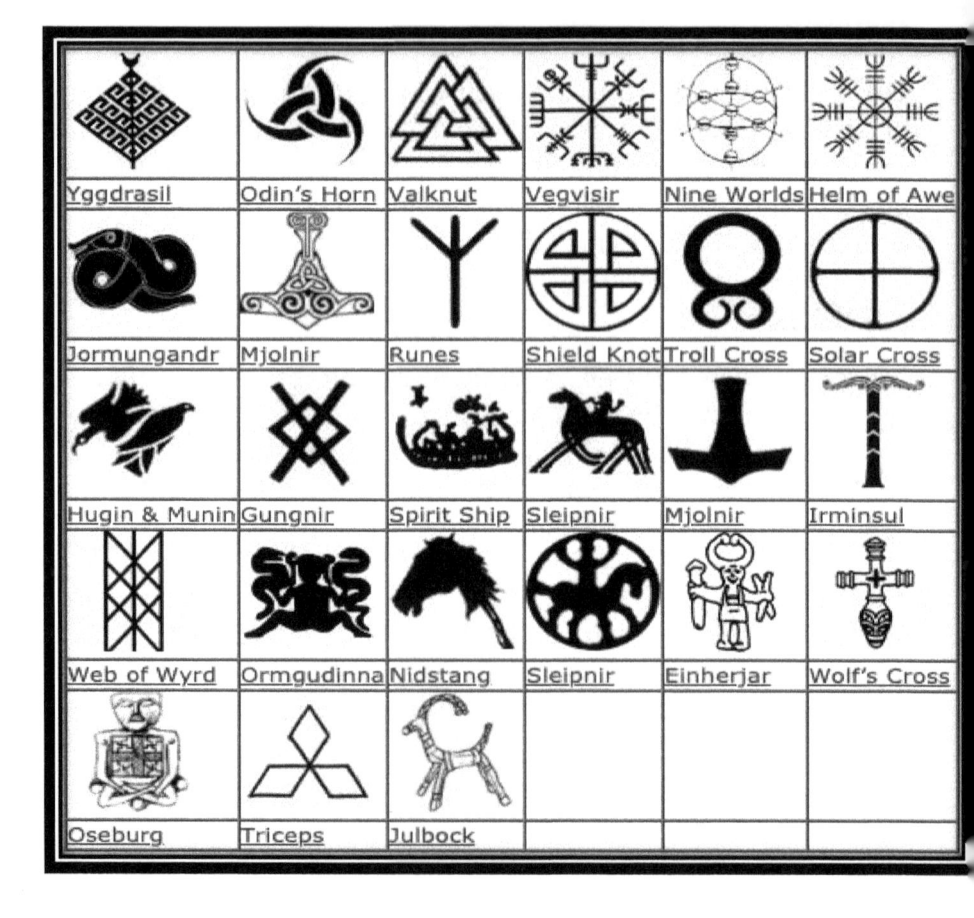

Yggdrasil	Odin's Horn	Valknut	Vegvisir	Nine Worlds	Helm of Awe
Jormungandr	Mjolnir	Runes	Shield Knot	Troll Cross	Solar Cross
Hugin & Munin	Gungnir	Spirit Ship	Sleipnir	Mjolnir	Irminsul
Web of Wyrd	Ormgudinna	Nidstang	Sleipnir	Einherjar	Wolf's Cross
Oseburg	Triceps	Julbock			

Chapter 7: The Nine Noble Virtues

The Nine Noble Virtues are a set of virtues that guide an individual's actions on Earth. First coined by Danish philosopher Søren Kierkegaard in 1843 to describe how one should live life with all its joys and pains, these nine tenets have since been adopted as moral codes throughout Scandinavian countries such as Denmark, Norway, and Sweden. The Nine Noble Virtues, Courage, Truth, Honor, Fidelity, Discipline, Hospitality, Self-Reliance, Industriousness, and Perseverance are the basis for an Asatruar's life. These virtues influence how you behave in different situations and affect your way of living as well.

Courage

Amongst the Nine Noble Virtues, courage is in many ways the most important as it forms the basis for all of the other virtues. The courage to face reality and your limitations and always be true to yourself and others are two key elements reflected within this virtue. A person who lacks courage has no value as a human being, according to Søren Kierkegaard, whether it be facing your inner demons or standing up for what you believe in; without having this trait, a person does not have true authenticity. This is one of those traits that good people often possess, as they can look danger in the eye even if they are scared out of their wits!

Necessary as this virtue does not always stand as the main component of an Asatruars life as many different situations cause a person to act out in doubt, fear and anxiety. This causes us to take on negative emotions rather than positive ones as courage by itself doesn't give you any directions; instead, it provides a framework for how one should face their fears and doubts. It is up to one's convictions as to whether they will embrace the virtues or not as there are no set rules of behavior within them as each situation requires its solution.

A man without courage is like a ship without sails or power as he becomes unable to function as part of his community; as an individual, he cannot go further than his threshold of bravery as he is practically as good as dead without this important quality.

The key takeaway from courage as a virtue is to face your fears and be true to oneself, as only then does one become courageous and able to live their life as they should have been living it all along!

TRUTH

The virtue of Truth as it stands in Asatru is an important part of embodying your beliefs and accepting others as they are. This broad interpretation allows for different people to see it both as a moral code and a divine law that cannot be broken or forsaken. To live an honest life is quite difficult as it means you have to face the consequences, whether good or bad when doing something you know is wrong and has possibly been warped by other people who don't necessarily share your views. Making promises which you can't keep, lying about certain things and having secrets will all come back to haunt you eventually, so it's best if one lives life as openly as possible as then there is no doubt as to what one believes in.

It is important to note the difference between honest and truth as it's possible to tell lies that seem truthful as many people will believe them if you give your words enough weight. Lying has become part of our society as we usually lie about pretty boring things such as how much money we make or where we got that beautiful gift from, but lies in these circumstances aren't a big deal unless they lead down a path of greater destruction such as lying about cheating on your spouse so that he doesn't find out.

The first of these lies are considered white lies where most people see them as harmless fibs, while the second type is as black as the deepest pit as they can destroy one's life and families.

As this virtue differs from person to person, it is important to understand that there isn't a one-size-fits-all answer. Everybody has their limitations, as some people may lack self-honesty and be too afraid to face reality. In contrast, others will run into trouble as they are unable to keep secrets for very long. These traits, of course, overlap with each other as self-honesty leads up to truthfulness, as the more you know about yourself, the easier it is for you to handle situations where lying would otherwise come upon your lips.

Honor

Honor is a big part of Asatru and consists of respect, courage, bravery, nobility, and generosity. Honor demands that we take responsibility for our actions daily. It also means knowing what you stand for and defending your principles. Your honor as a person is not something to be taken lightly as it can either elevate or destroy you and others.

Honor may also mean different things to each person as some see it as what you do while others will associate it with how you do something as your honor can be at stake depending on the circumstances. The latter has been referred to as personal honor, one's view of themselves and their actions. The former is more objective as it relies on how others perceive oneself and one's actions; this concept of Honor based on public opinion is known as reputation.

These two points are where most differences come from when it comes to Honor within Asatru, especially in modern times where most people choose whether they want to live as honorable as they can as they see it or if they'll rather go for the easy life as many of us have been conditioned to do as time has passed. We call character as it's the person you are and will continue to be after as long as you live. Hence, it's important to choose whether you want to be remembered as a coward who was afraid of facing reality or someone with great honor who stood up for their beliefs no matter the cost; there is nothing wrong with not choosing as your principles may change throughout your lifetime but make sure that when you have chosen you stick by them as Asatruar's dislike people who continually change sides at every turn just because something better came along.

Be true to thyself as that is what Honor demands as even if you can't see it yet; as long as you do the right thing for whatever reason, then your words shall be remembered as Asatruar's hold their Oath Breakers in contempt as without honor we are but animals!

FIDELITY

Fidelity is a virtue that many Asatru honor. The Norse gods often span multiple realities, and the goddesses are not always monogamous to their husbands either. However, this does not mean fidelity has no value in an Asatru's life; it means they do what makes them happy at any given time with whomever they want without feeling guilty for changing partners as we understand different people will suit our needs differently over time.

Fidelity can be seen as one of the virtues among some adherents of Asatro (Norse Religion). It doesn't matter if your deity spans across several realms or you're married to more than one person--you still commit yourself entirely when someone becomes part of your life, so there isn't anything wrong with not being exclusive as some claim as long as you're honest with yourself and your partner; it's as simple as that unless of course if you're in a relationship where sexual fidelity (sexual exclusivity) is part of the agreement as many modern relationships tend to be but then again, as we have stated earlier there are no real set rules when it comes to Asatro.

DISCIPLINE

Asatruars live in a world filled with great challenges and changes. With discipline, we can face these trials head-on while still living true to ourselves through our actions. When faced with adversity or setbacks, it's easy for us to give up hope when faced with adversity or setbacks because everything is so overwhelming that nothing seems possible anymore; yet if you're even slightly prepared beforehand, there will always be something worth fighting for. Discipline gives one the power to do so much more than one ever thought was possible! You may have started as someone who wanted only peace but found yourself thrust into battle when your lands were invaded by an enemy army years ago - now how would things be different had you not been able to find within yourself the discipline to fight as hard as you did through the long, harsh winters and many months of marching over rugged terrain? What if you found yourself sick or injured on the battlefield? How would having that essential strength of character keep fighting to help you recover from whatever ailed you?

HOSPITALITY

Hospitality is important for every culture and religion. It's even more important to those who follow a pagan path. The home is the center of the community. It provides safety for the children while they are growing up. Hospitality provides food, shelter, and care for all who visit. It also prevents outsiders from taking advantage of our generosity.

Be as generous as you can as far as your means as well as the limits of your home and family. However, never let an outsider be in control! Letting them think they can boss you around is a quick way to lose everything. You don't have any obligation to protect what is not yours either. If strangers come into the house for help and then decide they want to take over or worse - kill you and everyone else - that's their choice. You are under no obligation to die needlessly defending someone who isn't even related to you by blood. Also, remember that if people show up claiming hospitality, it is polite and respectful to ask if they are honest, as is their right to question you.

Be a good guest as well as a good host. To be an effective guest, first make sure that it's okay before asking for anything from the host and thanking them for everything they do, whether they offer special things or not. Greeting the people who live there and getting acquainted with them will help smooth over any bumps in your stay, as well as provide some additional support should something happen while you're visiting (like hunting, fishing, etc.). A guest doesn't humiliate his family or hurt anyone else staying there unless he leaves his free will and does so without causing trouble beforehand.

Self-Reliance

Self-reliance is a key part of the Asatruar faith. This includes personal responsibility and honor to oneself, family, kin, and the community. Asatruars are expected to be independent in thought and action. They should take responsibility for their own lives and well-being--to stand on one's own feet in times of hardship or need, to pursue one's goals with honest work and creativity. It's also about being ready for emergencies by maintaining a good quality of life that can withstand disaster/adversity.

Self-reliance is a core value in Asatru because it ties into many other values. Independence defines who you are, which means your actions are based on your principles instead of what you think society expects from you, as it does with people who are not Asatru. Having self-reliance allows Asatruars to create their own lives and follow their dreams without fear of persecution or lack of resources. Being Asatru also promotes the importance of a strong family and an honorable leader in charge who cares for his people as a whole and not just one section over another.

Self-reliance is important as an Asatruar because, without it, you cannot be successful on your own, which means as long as you keep yourself together with proper shelter, food (and water), clothing, and whatever other necessities needed to run a comfortable household then it's fine if you decide to leave the area for work or anything else just as long as you don't drag others down with you by simply taking from them what they have through force or trickery.

They help themselves first, then the community as a whole.

INDUSTRIOUSNESS

Industriousness is a core value for Asatru. It means that one should get out and do something to better their lives. Industriousness ties into many other values. Asatruars are industrious because they ensure that they have what they need to survive, such as food or shelter.

Being industrious is important in the Asatru faith because it shows your devotion to your god and the approach you take to live. Your hard work will be rewarded with success (regardless of how much time it takes), and all those who show the same dedication will benefit from your success and contribute to the Asatru community as a whole.

If you don't work, you're not contributing to the Asatru community or providing anything for yourself and your family.

Perseverance

Perseverance is a key part of the Asatru faith. It's about acting in an honorable way, trying to trust someone, and resisting difficulties. This includes not giving up when life gets hard--to keep on going through anything because being persevering is something that will never be taken away from you.

Being Asatru means persevering because it helps with many other values such as Honor and Courage. Perseverance allows people to work with what they've got and still show honor even if others see giving up as acceptable in certain scenarios. Basking in what others view as a loss gives you more control over your destiny. It allows you to continue without giving up, which is important for any person who strives to succeed in Asatru as long as you don't fall into the same traps as those who gave up and keep others around you from doing so as well.

Perseverance is also nice when it comes to dealing with other people (friends or enemies) because if they can see that despite what they do to deter you from your goals, then there's no way for them to win against you which means all conflict/disputes will be resolved in a peaceful and honorable manner.

Asatruars take personal responsibility for learning the ways that life works and for living in such a way that others can rely on them as well as being able to rely on others.

The Nine Sacred Virtues are powerful and inspirational; however, they are not meant for everyone. They are made to benefit those who strive to follow them by allowing them to rise above the mundane existence of modern life, which is full of chaos, confusion, and torment as deal as much as possible with those who are Asatru as well as being willing to help others as best as they can by offering their possessions as well as assistance in times of need. The Nine Sacred Virtues are meant for those who choose Asatru, those who have no other choice but to follow them, and those who want to learn more about the past because there is a lot to learn from it.

The Nine Sacred Virtues not only affect one's life on earth; however, they also affect what may come afterward as an aftereffect. They build up a person's good karma, which has been known to help open doors once spent time in Valhalla, where you will eventually reach Frigga's Hall.

Conclusion

Many people are turning to ancient pre-Christian and pre-Islamic traditions in quest of more significant meaning in a world where technology is taking over and cityscapes are becoming the reality for more and more people. These traditions have the potential to teach us how to reconnect with nature: how to interact with the ocean, the mountains, the streams, the weeds, the trees, the fields, the sky, and the sun—all the things in this world that, if you take a moment and pay attention, remind you of their importance and the fact that you could not exist without them. The knowledge that our ancient predecessors once communicated with a world full of animals, plants, fish, birds—and life—is what draws us to these traditional practices. We believe that if we can just tune in—if we can only grasp the old language that was lost with the translations, modernization, and globalization—we have better odds for a greater tomorrow.

The term Asatru is an Old Norse word for "belief in the gods." The religion of Asatru has its roots all the way back to when our ancestors worshipped a pantheon of deities. It was practiced by Vikings, among other people, until Christianity came into power and outlawed it. Today there are practitioners who continue their tradition as well as new followers joining each day!

Asatru is a polytheistic religion, meaning it worships multiple deities. It also puts great emphasis on honoring ancestors and respecting the land we live upon. Since Asatru places so much importance on the natural world, many of its followers are environmentally conscious.

Asatru has such a beautiful history and tradition. It teaches us the importance of honoring both our ancestors and the land we live upon. Asatru can be practiced by individuals as well as families to help guide them through life's difficulties. Whether you become an active follower or simply appreciate its deep meaning, I believe anyone would benefit from learning about and understanding Asatru.

Asatru offers the same opportunity to everyone. It's not only for those who are raised in it—although they may understand it more from childhood exposure—but also for anyone willing to learn and experience its culture. Asatru can be practiced by anyone of any race, creed, gender, sexuality or nationality. Although there are some beliefs that differentiate Asatru from other religions, most people find themselves agreeing with many of its values.

In modern times, practitioners pay homage to their gods through private rituals at home or outdoors on sacred ground in natural settings where they can feel connected with nature. Asatru encourages personal growth by tapping into one's inner strength; it offers guidance for those who are lost, confused, or seeking spiritual enlightenment while providing grounding during difficult times—like illness, death of loved ones, etc.—and guidelines as one moves forward into the future such as marriage decisions which often have significant impacts on family members' lives down generations

There is nothing wrong with embracing traditions outside of mainstream religions. There are so many nuances to all of them that it's easy for differing opinions to exist without any animosity or hatred present. We need to remember that we're all people trying to live beautiful lives and respect one another while doing so. Life is too short—we should be working together, not against each other!

We hope this book has provided you with a basic understanding of Asatru, an opportunity to learn more and perhaps even find your own place in the tradition!

Chapter 8: Cosmology—The Tree Of Life And The Nine Worlds

This chapter is dedicated to the Yggdrasil and the nine worlds of Asatru cosmology. We will explore what each world means in relation to our lives, how we can interact with them, and what that might look like. All nine worlds exist around a huge tree called Yggdrasil, which has three roots. One root connects it to the land of ice, one is connected to the land of fire, and one enters into Niflheim (the world of no light). These roots all connect at different points at the surface level and go down deep into the Earth's core, where they are intertwined in a single root system, so they grow together.

Yggdrasil

The Yggdrasil is the World Tree that connects all of existence as we know it. It was first believed to be a mythological tree but has since been found in various religions and cultures throughout history on many different continents worldwide.

The ancient Greeks, for example, had an idea for this massive cosmic tree called "the Ash" or "Yggdrasil" which held up three celestial spheres: one populated by humans; another occupied with stars/celestial bodies; and finally, branches reaching into every region below them where four stags graze on its foliage representing life's ills (hunger, strife, etc.). The Vedic lore also includes references to such trees connecting earthlings (man) to the heavens (gods' dwelling).

Yggdrasil translates literally as "Steed of Yggr" or "Odin's Horse." This mythological tree is associated with many things, including knowledge since its branches allow people from all across the world access to information concerning their gods as well as themselves; wisdom due to being able to see into pasts and futures through these roots; magic because even though this creature can be killed by using one of three methods, such death will result in rebirth within nine days at most and it will grow again.

It is said that a dragon named Nidhoggr (Nidhugr) lives at the base of this tree, gnawing away on its roots which causes Yggdrasil to wither as time goes by.

The mighty Yggdrasil stands tall above all other trees. The tree is so strong it supports the whole of Heaven and Earth with three roots, one in Asgard where gods reside, another on Jotunheim for giants to live upon, and a third rooted deep within Helheim for wicked souls that must be punished by eternal torture.

The World Tree is an integral part of Ragnarok's tale. Only two humans, Lif and Lifthrasir, have survived the Ragnarok, according to Norse mythology. By hiding under Yggdrasil's branches and consuming the dew on the World Tree leaves, these two humans would be able to avoid the worst of the fighting.

THE NINE WORLDS OF ASATRU

Asatru cosmology revolves around the Yggdrasil World Tree. Around this magnificent tree are the different realms created. This chapter deals with Yggdrasil and the nine cosmological worlds of Asatru.

The ancient Nordic people did not see the universe as consisting solely of the Earth, surrounded by the heavens above and the underworld or hell underneath. The cosmos, according to Asatru, is a complicated system with many realms and planes, including the human domain. All of the planes of creation were linked to one another.

Muspelheim, the blazing world of fire in the south, migrated north to meet Niflheim, the freezing realm, before the beginning of time. Their powers merged when they met in Ginnungagap or the yawning nothingness. The union of Muspelheim and Niflheim produced two beings: Ymir (who we discussed earlier in this chapter) and Audhumla, a massive primeval cow.

Buri was born after the primordial cow licked the ice. Marriages among these primordial beings and Ymir's sexless reproduction resulted in multiple creatures until Ymir was killed. The cosmos was constructed from his bodily parts by three heavenly beings: Odin Villi, and Ve. The World Tree and the nine worlds were part of the cosmos built from Ymir's body parts. The nine worlds were supported by the World Tree, Yggdrasil, and were separated by enormous distances.

Rivers, valleys, hills, and mountains separated the nine worlds, and the World Tree's bark formed a barrier between them. According to Norse paganism, the entire cosmos is much larger than the nine worlds centered on Yggdrasil. Beyond the nine worlds' perimeter, there exist unknown worlds.

ALFHEIM
The Realm Of The Light Elves

Alfheim is the realm of light, home to those who embody virtues such as beauty and wisdom. It lies in the sky above Midgard, where there are no stars or sun. The light elves live here without feeling cold or hot, day or night, for that matter. They spend their time playing games with each other and maintaining a state of purity at all times by bathing in pure waters from springs on its land. The gods have granted Alfheim this near-perfect living environment because they see it as an example of what should be done when inhabiting Midgard below them. These elves are not allowed to leave Alfheim unless invited by someone from Asgard if wars must be fought against giants (jotnar) or other forces of destruction.

Alfheim is the home of the elves. They are said to be drawn in by their beautifully designed landscapes and towering trees, which they cherish as part of Mother Nature's legacy. The natives who live there maintain a healthy balance with nature, guiding them through life like nobody else could have done for them before their arrival centuries ago.

Elves are tall, thin beings with a long lifespan (up to 800 years), and they are physically weaker than humans. Elves have pointed ears that can be seen from afar, and their sharp features help them stand out among the people who live in Midgard below them.

Elves live in houses for centuries before moving on as the world changes around them. They do not need to eat, but they enjoy doing so because food is an ancient tradition among elves that connects us to Mother Earth's wisdom.

ASGARD
THE REALM OF THE AESIR TRIBE

Asgard is the realm of the Aesir gods and goddesses. According to Norse mythology, Asgard is the home of all that is good in the world, such as peace, justice, honor, and truth. It is ruled by Odin and protected by Thor.

The word "Asgard" means fortress or stronghold. The inhabitants live within a large enclosure with golden walls that allow them to see into every part of their land - hence the name.

The realm of the Aesir gods is a shining city with golden rooftops and glittering rivers where all manner of creatures frolic in the waters. The goddess Frigga resides here, and her gardeners are said to coax flowers from even the rockiest ground.

The gleaming citadel that houses Asgard's deities sits atop a high mountain ridge, framed by two mountains on either side as if they were its guardsmen or sentinels. It rests at peace throughout eternity between battles against demons and giants who would harm the fragile humanity below them.

The two most important halls in Asgard are Vingolf, where the goddesses meet, and Gladsheim, where the gods meet.

The gods and goddesses walk on the Bifrost bridge every day to hold their deliberations under the shade of Yggdrasil, which connects the mortal realm, Midgard, to the gods' bright world, Asgard. The Aesir built the rainbow bridge, and the deity Heimdall serves as its guardian. The roaring fire represented the red color of the rainbow, which served as protection against the giants. The bridge is destined to be destroyed at the end of the world, Ragnarok.

Muspelheim
The World Of The Primal Fire
And The Home Of The Fire Giants

Muspelheim is a dangerous yet beautiful place. The fire giants that live here must have fiery souls to survive the blistering heat and treacherous terrain of this world's endless deserts. Many battles were fought on its sands because it has been said that Muspelheim will outlive Midgard when Ragnarok comes around!

According to Norse mythology, Muspelheim was created due to a rebellion against Odin during his reign over Asgard. It exists somewhere in the universe but not near any other inhabited regions.

The realms of Muspelheim and Niflheim (the realm of ice) came together to form the first being: Ymir. Comets, stars, and planets are said to have been generated by sparks from this world. Muspelheim fire giants are said to be fighting the gods in Ragnarok, according to some Norse mythology texts.

Niflheim
The Domain Of The Primeval Snow And The World Of Mists

Niflheim is the world of perpetual snow where everything has been turned into ice. Mountains are covered in layers upon layers of white, untouched by any other color or life form, and rivers have frozen to an icy mass that can shatter like glass at a single touch. This land seems desolate, but animals live within its depths; you may see them as their blue eyes peer out from behind rock sides or glimpse them running over mountainside slopes before they vanish again so quickly, it's hard to tell what animal was even present for more than a second.

Niflheim is one of the nine worlds in Norse mythology, and it's considered to be linked with death. If you die on Earth, your spirit may go to Niflheim, or Hel, depending on who you are and what kind of life you led. The goddess Hel rules over this land, a desolate place of misery, frost, and ice.

Niflheim is separated into several sub-realms, one of which is dedicated to gods and heroes. The goddess Hel presides over the celebrations for the gods and heroes in this sub-realm. Another level of Niflheim is reserved for the sick, elderly, and those who cannot die in glory. Those who die in glory go straight to Asgard's Valhalla.

The lowest sub-realm of Niflheim is comparable to the Christian hell, where the wicked will languish for all eternity. Niflheim is near the river Hvergelmir, which means "stream that bubbles and boils," and the darkened hall, or Nastrand, which means "corpse strands," and is located underneath the third root of Yggdrasil.

JOTUNHEIM
THE LAND OF GIANTS AND THE JOTNAR

Jotunheim is the land of giants and jotnar. It lies just north of Hel, home to those who have died in unspeakably violent ways. It is a place where trolls dwell and also houses frost giants like Thrym. The giants pose a serious threat to the people of Midgard and the gods of Asgard. The Iving River separates Asgard and Jotunheim. Utgard is the most important city in the land of the giants.

Utgard was the giants' main fortress, from which Loki governed the kingdom. Loki was a cunning, deadly, and strong giant who appeared as Thor's ally and partner in various legends. Utgard, which means "the world beyond the enclosure," is inhabited by malevolent beings. Asgard and Midgard are portrayed as areas shared by gods and humans, with both having access to them, whereas Utgard is seen as a divider, resembling an ocean or river.

Thrymheim (Thyai's home) and Gastropnir are two other notable locales in Jotunheim (the dwelling of Menglad). The Jarnvid, or "ironwood," is also housed there. Jotunheim is located north of Midgard, according to mythology.

Helheim
The Realm Of The Dead

The realm or abode of the dead is known as Helheim or Hel. It is the lowest realm of the nine worlds, ruled by the goddess Hel or Hella. It is close to Niflheim, resting well underneath the Yggdrasil. Helheim is not entirely evil and dark. Some areas resemble an afterlife paradise full of light and happiness, while others are dismal and bleak.

Hel is also not a place of torment. It is primarily a resting place for the souls of the deceased. It's haunted by the specters of souls who died in vain or lived a life of sin. Helheim is also the home of souls who have failed to keep the pledges they have made throughout their lifetimes.

Helheim is accessible by three portals: The Hell Way, the Highway to Hell or Helvergr; Gjoll, the Blood River; and Gnipahellier or the Overhanging Cave.

Hel's Gate (Helgrind) or Corpse Gate (Nagrind) is the entrance to Hel, and it is guarded by a giantess, Modgud, and her giant hound, Garmr. Hel's gates are to the south, away from Asgard's, which are to the north. Gjoll, the river of blood that surrounds Hel, is very cold and strewn with knives.

Walking across a bridge guarded by a giantess is the only way to get across the river. According to Norse pagan beliefs, a living person walking on the bridge would make such a tremendous noise that it would appear as if a thousand men were attempting to cross it, while a dead person might cross the bridge without making a sound.

The goddess Hel's home, known as Evdinir or "misery," is located in the northern half of Hel. The goddess Hel's palace is surrounded by a wall known as the "falling peril" or Fallanda

Forad. Kvalheim, the land of retribution for the wicked, is located underneath Hel's mansion and made of adders or snakes. Wicked people are brought here to be poisoned by the snakes' venom.

VANAHEIM
THE KINGDOM OF THE VANIR TRIBE

Vanaheim is one of the highest levels in Norse paganism's cosmology, and it is home to the Vanir gods and goddesses. It is very close to Asgard. Vanaheim is also known as the home of the fertility goddesses of the Earth. The Vanir gods are thought to be more kind and benign than the Aesir gods, who are more passionate and pugnacious.

Njord, Freyr, and Freya are the three most important deities of Vanaheim. Vanaheim, like Asgard, is full of majestic houses and palaces. Njord was born in Vanaheim, and he will return after Ragnarok as one of the few gods and goddesses predicted to survive the end of the world.

SVARTALFHEIM—THE KINGDOM OF THE DWARVES AND BLACK ELVES

The land of the dark elves is Svartalfheim (the light elves live in Alfheim). In Norse mythology, black or dark elves are known as dokkalfar. The dark elves, like the trolls, are linked to "daveves" or "dvergar." According to certain tales, this world could be accessible through the caves in Midgard.

Svartalfheim, home to the dwarves and black elves, is a kingdom shrouded in darkness. Dwarves are masters of their crafts, while elves hide away secrets that they refuse to let anyone know. The only thing more mysterious than the inhabitants of this kingdom appears to be its location on Earth, as no one has ever seen Svartalfheim before.

Midgard
The Human Realm

Midgard is a realm in the middle, so it's often referred to as Middle Earth. In this world of humans, you can find all sorts of locations, from mountains and valleys to waterfalls and forests - everything that one might expect when they think about Midgard.

Between Helheim (hell or the underworld) and Asgard, there is a world known as Midgard (the heavens or the upper world). As a result, Midgard is a part of a triad that includes the upper realm known as the Heavens, Earth in the middle realm, and the Underworld in the lower realm.

Ymir, the primal living being, was used to create Midgard. Midgard is connected to Asgard via Bifrost, a rainbow bridge guarded by Heimdall. Midgard is surrounded by a vast ocean, which is home to Jormungandr, the great snake. It's so big and long that it completely encircles Midgard and bites its tail in the process.

Because Thor is the son of the Earth Goddess, he has vowed to protect the people of Midgard. He became Asgard's self-appointed protector because he was an Aesir. As a result, Thor was a powerful protector of Midgard and Asgard from marauding beings who sought to harm the two worlds closest to Thor's heart.

According to Norse mythology, Midgard's annihilation was due to Ragnarok. Jormungandr rose from the vast seas surrounding Midgard, intending to poison the land and water with its venom. The sea slapped the shore. Almost all of life in Midgard was destroyed in the final battle, and the sea swallowed the Earth.

Innangard And Utangard

Geographical areas and psychological conditions are often classified as innangard or utangard in Norse mythology and religion.

In Norse culture, there are two types of worlds. One is innangard if it's orderly, civilized, and law-abiding. The other type of world is utangard, which means chaotic or wild in their perspective beliefs system.

Innangard is the orderly, civilized, law-abiding world. There are many well-defined rules for social interaction here, and they follow set guidelines accordingly if you plan on interacting with those who live there. For example, rules such as how to act at feasts or during rituals where various behaviors are expected depending on the type of ritual, which group or family one belongs to (there's more than one), or even according to gender roles; these details all have their place within the innangard system.

The innangard system also has rules for how one interacts with the natural world, such as harvesting fruit from trees or what types of plants are best suited for different purposes.

However, to stay within this system, it's necessary to be a part of certain groups that offer security and protection. There are also ways that you can live independently if you so choose but doing so will involve taking some major risks because there is no way others will automatically protect you against all dangers should they arise. Innangard doesn't allow those who don't belong there into their territories without consequences being enforced upon them by its members.

Utangard, on the other hand, is often described as chaotic or wild because it has very few laws governing social interactions between individuals. Utangard is a place for those who want to live without restrictions, where the individual is free from any societal codes or conventions.

Some people believe utangard to be more dangerous than innangard due to this lack of rules and regulations that ensure safety. The dangers involved in living outside society are much more serious because there's no one watching over anyone else; however, others claim utangard offers protection against innangard's tyranny if you're willing to take the risk and decide not to abide by their laws.

In medieval Iceland, the distinction between the innangard and the utangard was mapped in a series of social, political, economic, and faith customs, just as in other Germanic societies. The Christian influence remained nominal or non-existent. The fences that enclosed farms, for example, have a cosmological/magical purpose, which is not only indistinguishable from their more immediate practical objective: they were there not only to keep animals in the enclosure but also to maintain trolls, giants, and other hostile inhabitants of the wild. Fences have marked a border between the two separate states.

Law has been much in the same vein. The Icelanders of the Medieval period called their society "our law," which shows that the "law" and "society" were two expressions. They called this "our law." Law was a psychical enclosure that separated the social, the innangard, from the antisocial, utangard. Therefore, it was outlawing punishment for particularly abominable crimes, whereby one loses one's civil rights and could be killed in sight without any legal effect. Due to the crime, the outlaw was an utangard rather than an innangard, and as the criminal had no control of society will thus be deprived of the protection of society. This transition from being a civilized to a wild person is evident from the very words related to outlawing: forestry is known as "going into the forest," and the outlaw is called a "forest man." It was often appropriate for outlaws to flee as far from human homes as possible for obvious reasons.

The distinction between innangard and utangard has been drawn in the spiritual cosmology of Germanic art. Three of the nine worlds have the suffix "-gard" and are quintessentially innangard or utangard places: Midgard, Asgard, and Utgard (another name for Jotunheim). The first two are inalienable worlds: Midgard (the middle enclosure at least in parts of Asgard) is the world of human civilization, the world of the fields and the fences, and the enclosure of the Aesir. Both realms need to defend themselves against attacks by Jotunheim/lawless Utgard's residents, the giants. (Indeed, "Utgard" is just another "utangard" version of the word.).

However, the utangard is not regarded as entirely destructive or negative. Men and women sometimes went into the utangard deliberately for a specific constructive purpose. The process of starting a warband (a particular type of military society) involved, for example, spending time alone in the countryside to overcome a situation of extreme vulnerability. If it were a totem animal, the candidate would probably have learned how the animal was to be semi-united with the animal and the warband itself by extension. From these tests, the new warband member gained strength and understanding and, paradoxically, would then use the chaotic and antisocial skills and pressures to serve society.

Maybe then Odin, patron god of these elite warriors, has a mother-like giant and is, therefore, a half-giant himself. It's no surprise. Although he is the chief of the Aesir, Odin has several extremely utangard characteristics, including tendencies to assume a female role in some instances, a fondness for seeking giants to gain their immense knowledge, a reputation as a whimsical and disloyal trickster, and sometimes a more significant concern for their personal development and power than well-being. Of course, these features did not prevent the heathen Germanic people from adoring him fervently and people of a certain temper even emulating him.

More generally, the Aesir-giant relationship is highly ambivalent. Even Thor, famed for ruthless defense against the evil will of giants against Asgard and Midgard, is a three-quarters giant himself.

As Henning Kure's analysis of the Norse showed, the utangard was seen as a unique raw power source channeled to building innangard quests. Just as the cry is the source of every discourse, the order can only be formed out of the primal mess; therefore, the former's continued existence depends on the latter.

Chapter 9: Runes, Charms, And Magic

What kinds of esoteric practices do heathens engage in? There are many things, but two things stand out most prominently. One is working with runes, while the other is performing a seidh.

Heathenry has its system of what can be called the esoteric arts - a term used to describe the secret magical or spiritual knowledge available only to the initiates in an organization. Two prominent practices include using runes and doing seidh.

Initially, runes were only used as a means of communication. However, later on in time, people found that the world was full of magic, and they wanted to explore it more. Many do this through experimenting with rune talismans or charms for protection against evil spirits or forces like death.

Historically, runes were used to denote ownership and often tell a story, too.

Runes have been found on everything from merchants' tags, which ensured that they knew who their product belonged to in the event it was stolen or lost, all the way up to the vast stone monuments where runes recorded historical events.

First off, while runes were used traditionally by people from Scandinavian cultures, they can now be found around the world in places far beyond their birthplaces. Interpreting runes can occur during a personal ritual alone or a ceremony with a group using rune stones, which have been around since the 17th century in Iceland. One popular way to read them is to cast three runes out onto a cloth laid flat on a table. The first symbol thrown relates to something that has happened before the current moment; next up will represent what's going on now; lastly, you may see an insight into what lies ahead. Once these meanings are identified, they're often translated into another form, like pictures or words, so that we can better understand their meaning.

Odin was the father of runes in mythological lore. He is often depicted with a spear, wearing an animal skin and having one eye sacrificed to gain knowledge of reading mystical symbols from which all life springs forth - including man's fate on Earth.

The Younger and Elder Futharks are the two main sets of rune rows left for us. The runes in the younger set were created around 400 AD, while the older ones date back as far as 2500 BCE.

The main difference is that the younger rune row contains only sixteen letters, whereas the older version contains twenty-four additional symbols, each with a different meaning.

Each rune has its symbol or sound linked with it as a type of writing. For example, Inguz is frequently used to represent the diphthong "ng." In addition, each rune has a single-word connotation, a mnemonic employed by skalds and anyone who needed to recall the runes and their meanings.

Rune Meaning in the Elder Futhark

Fehu

Fehu represents the wealth of a household and its distribution amongst kin. It also means gold, which can cause strife between members who want it for themselves. Therefore, the brightness of the flood tide might be interpreted as an omen that could lead to riches or disaster.

Fehu's meaning encompasses both positive and negative aspects: on the one hand, Fehu may bring prosperity to households by allocating different amounts to each member; on the other hand, wealthy families with excessive greed will use up their resources, such as water, until they are gone forever, just as those caught in a flooded tide have little chance of surviving if not saved quickly enough.

Uruz

Uruz is hard to translate, but it has been likened to the Aurochs, an ancient breed of cattle. Meaning "the good bull," it symbolizes bravery in battle or strength on the farm.

What does Uruz mean? This particular runic letter stands for robust agriculture that has since fallen into extreme negligence. Poor farming practices have led us from bountiful harvests into famine-ravaged fields where we can barely raise enough crops to feed our livestock.

Thurisaz

Thurisaz is a venomous thorn that afflicts women, causing them to suffer from pain. The children born from these unions are known as thursar, and they are not well received by their mothers because they will be reminded of how they were wronged.

Thurisaz was considered to cause severe illness in females due to its intense stinging nature. In addition, it symbolized physical suffering or spiritual anguish, such as childbirth pains for new mothers who could never forget what happened when Thurizas inflicted itself upon their unborn babies with full force.

It also represents those times when someone feels betrayed and injured at the hands of another person who should have cared for them but instead caused emotional harm.

Ansuz

The Ansuz rune symbolizes wisdom and the scabbard for swords, which makes it perfect to wear on your neck when you enter battle. Odin himself wore this symbol around his neck as he led Asgard into a war against giants like Ymir or Jormungandr.

This symbol protects its bearer from harm in any way that they need it most, whether physically or mentally with their opponent during battle.

Raido

The Raido rune is, in many ways, the embodiment of a traveler's journey. It represents happiness and freedom but also weariness. Travelers often scratched it to inscribe into stones near rest sites as they made their way on foot or horseback through forests where no paths existed.

The Raido rune has two meanings that are entirely dependent on each other: the first refers to blissful comfort while traveling long distances, such as when you finally arrive home after being gone for too long; the second relates to roughness due to hardship from travel, similar if not equivalent to what horses experience during difficult journeys, such as pulling wagons over rocky roads.

Kenaz

The Kenaz rune is associated with a light that burns brightly. It can represent misfortune as well. However, the shine of this torchlight should not be feared.

Kenaz means "torch," and it delivers brightness both figuratively and literally in many ways: from its illumination to providing counsel for those who are lost or seeking wisdom. Moreover, Kenaz's knowledge frequently fuels an inner fire, which then turns into a physical flame - so why be afraid of what could potentially purify you?

Gebo

Gebo is a rune of giving and receiving. It symbolizes a gift that benefits both parties, which can be physical or spiritual. It also represents survival as it brings luck to its holder during difficult times with gifts from others when they need them most.

The Gebo rune signifies how we give back what has been given to us - not just materially, but emotionally too. By paying kindness forward and returning favors, our community remains strong because everyone relies on each other for support at some point in their lives.

Wunjo

The Wunjo rune stands for joy, prosperity, and bliss. Therefore, this symbol is strongly associated with success in all areas of life, such as love, business, and more.

The Wunjo rune has many meanings, which include happiness or luck. Still, it's most commonly seen to represent success in every area from career to relationships because when combined with other runes like Eoh (prosperity), Ingwaz (fertility), or Pertho (fruitfulness), they form what is called "kenning" that can be used to achieve one's goals or nurture the desired outcome.

Hagalaz

Hagalaz is the rune of hail, which represents an event that can be as destructive and cold as a blizzard.

Hagalaz symbolizes the purity and power of winter's most fearsome natural phenomenon: ice. Fighting against it is futile; only by respecting its might can you hope to live through its wrath.

Nauthiz

As a runic symbol, Nauthiz represents hard work and an oppressive force that can be conquered with effort and patience.

Isa

The Isa rune is a potent symbol that suggests either danger or opportunity. One interpretation of the ice rune could be in terms of an unanticipated bridge across cold waters, like when two glaciers make contact and create a path for travelers to cross over into new territory - but it can also represent treacherous icy undercurrents that are waiting just below the surface.

The Isa rune has been interpreted as dangerous ice escapes found on sea routes near Greenland or Scandinavia, which were once perilous passages through beautiful but deadly landscapes.

Jera

This symbol of agriculture and harvest is known for kindness in ensuring that all crops are fruitful.

In the depths of winter, Jera brings warmth and light. The long days allow plants to grow healthier than they ever could in spring or autumn.

Jera is responsible for all that we take for granted: the generous harvest or a ripe field ready with produce from sun-ripened tomatoes to plump peaches.

Eiwaz

The Eiwaz rune represents the yew tree, and this striking symbol has been used in Norse mythology to describe Odin's one-eyed horse Sleipnir and J.R.R Tolkien for Gandalf's staff.

The meaning of Eiwaz is not fully known, although many scholars believe it stands for "tranquility" or "a hidden force." It can also be interpreted that with peace comes progress because, without tranquility, life could not exist.

Perthro

The Perthro rune is traditionally associated with a dice cup, sport, and laughter. The Norse believed that the power of this stone created luck in games such as dice or playing board games, which has carried over to modern culture, where gambling is considered unethical.

The magic of this rune stone brings good fortune because it promised prosperity in any game played by throwing them into a bowl called perthr (or "dice container").

Algiz

The Algiz rune symbol is a picture of an elk's grass-cutting antlers, and it has profound healing properties for cuts.

The Algiz rune's design is inspired by a deer's sharpened horns, with each one cut to represent slashing through hard things like blades of grass or even bones to get at what lies beneath them. This alludes not only to how powerful this ancient Norse runic letter could be but also signifies just how far our ancestors were willing to go when they needed extra help getting out from under such burdens as sickness or injury.

Sowilo

Sowilo is the rune of victory and glory, representing light in all its forms.

Some believe that Sowilo represents a force for good intentions on Earth. However, it can best be described as an extension of divine energy to help promote growth among those who deserve it.

Tiwaz

The Tiwaz rune is the symbol of Tyr, a Norse god with ties to victory and justice. The meaning behind this formidable warrior's heritage can be seen in its association with warcraft.

Berkana

The Berkana rune is a sign of renewal, bringing life to the tree and giving it new hope.

While most trees are home to fruit that sustains them throughout their lives, birch trees instead feed on bark from other fallen logs to grow strong and healthy. The symbolism behind this can be interpreted as an act of rebirth: stripping away the old for something better.

Ehwaz

The Ehwaz rune has a deep connection to our animalistic, primal selves. It represents the union of two horses and is symbolic of those who have an innate power over others due to their intelligence and cunningness. The horse's speed is often used as a symbol in many cultures that follow this path, such as Hinduism, where it represents Shakti or God Shiva's force, purportedly responsible for his ability to transcend time itself.

The Ehwaz rune stands out from other symbols because it combines animals with nature; man is not solely reliant on what he can create but also relies upon what Mother Earth provides him with, like food, water, shelter, etc., much like how we rely on each other at times during challenging moments.

Mannaz

The Mannaz rune is symbolic of the increase in man's power and force on Earth. The symbol represents a person or human body, growing more potent over time with experience gained from hard work and companionship.

Laguz

The Laguz rune symbolizes a vast body of water. It can represent the sea, rivers, or the ocean, and the streams and rivers that flow into them. The symbolic meaning is associated with any event where something comes together as an unstoppable force, such as a fire extinguished by water to quench its flames forever.

The Laguz rune represents not just one thing, but many things: it stands for both oceans and smaller bodies of waters like ponds; it signifies surges from falls too small to deserve their name yet impressive enough nonetheless. Finally, this letter has deep ties with those who work within these horizons - sailors are often seen wearing amulets containing runes carved on wood which serve primarily for protection against bad weather conditions at sea. These amulets are also said to help in a storm at sea or even some form of mystical attack.

Inguz

The Inguz rune is a symbol of Frey, the first one seen by the East Danes. God's power and wisdom are depicted in this iconic sign that depicts fertility, sex appeal, and love.

Dagaz

The Dagaz rune represents both the sun and a benefit to all. The ancient Norse word "dagr" means "day," while "dag" is an old English word for "a feast or festival." This meaning can be extended in many ways, but one thing that stands out as necessary is social gatherings.

The Dagaz rune symbolizes the sun shining upon us and signifies the benefits that often come from contact with others in person. It simultaneously embodies the aspects of community building through time spent celebrating holidays together.

Othila

The Othila rune is used in divination to represent a person's ancestral land, which is extremely valuable at any time.

The Othilia rune represents one's native and ancestral land - an important factor for anyone seeking knowledge about oneself or their future endeavors.

To conclude, runes are a type of alphabet that can be used for divination. The interpretation is highly personal because it depends on their personality and lifestyle habits to connect with their meaning. Runes may represent certain letters, but they also have symbolic connotations depending on which rune you're interpreting from your reading experience or study sessions, making them very versatile in how one should approach studying them.

The interpretation of rune stones varies greatly among practitioners. They choose interpretations based on what resonates most deeply within each person's soul while meditating, researching mystical texts about the history behind these ancient symbols, and developing healthy daily routines so one can more easily tap into the subconscious mind.

The word rune is derived from an Anglo-Saxon word meaning "mystery." The runes were ancient symbols used as a secret language to keep important information hidden from enemies or other people who weren't trustworthy enough with such knowledge, such as when discussing battles and strategy plans on the battlefield.

Runes are powerful tools because they can create change by focusing on our intentions, shaping our thoughts on paper while writing spells through letters and words, and putting positive energy into things we want to manifest. They also help protect us against harmful energies, communicate messages of magic power throughout the different realms (such as the human world, the underworld, and the world of gods), access higher levels of consciousness, and develop our spiritual awareness.

Runes are a potent tool to use for transformation. Different types of runes correspond with different aspects of life, such as love, magic, protection, success, etc. But they can all be used for both benevolent and malevolent purposes, depending on how you choose to use them.

RUNE CASTING TECHNIQUES

SINGLE RUNE CAST

A single rune cast is the most basic summary of any scenario and is used to answer yes or no questions; the answer is found in the rune drawn. See the meaning of each rune above for a more in-depth study.

Urd—Verdandi—Skuld

Heathens believe that the past is permanent, and so they are constantly learning from it. However, the present moment is ever-changing because we can always grow or change in response to what is happening now.

Heathenism shows deep respect for all four dimensions of time: past (permanent), present (ever-changing), future (conditional), with an emphasis on the suitable action during each one at any given point in space/time continuum.

Heathenism views time as an arrow, always moving forward and never back, with each moment presenting its own set of new possibilities. There is only one certainty in their future - either good or bad, depending on their actions today (rather than tomorrow).

It's helpful to understand this concept before talking about this rune casting technique.

Don't think in terms like "past, present, and future" when casting this rune row. Instead, think of the runes as "what has passed," "what is becoming," and "what will become, considering the current condition."

The "urd" rune is the first to be drawn, representing the past, the things that have already happened and can no longer be changed.

The "verdandi" rune is drawn next to represent what is still affecting us in some way. Thus, it means the actions we can take in the present.

"Skuld" is the third rune pulled. It represents the future, what will happen if we don't take any action. It symbolizes what has not yet happened but could, given certain conditions, remain as they are in the present or if something new that changes those conditions happens.

After pulling all three runes, a series of events may be deduced to lead to the "skuld" rune, representing the outcome.

THROWING OR CASTING METHOD

When looking for a more complex response to any question, this strategy is useful. Get your runes out of the bag or container they're in. Concentrate your thoughts on the problem at hand. Stir the runes slowly as you do so. Grab whatever runes you have in your hand and toss them onto a cloth or other casting surface when the time is appropriate. Leave the other runes in the bag; these are the ones that are most relevant to the scenario. Take a look at the general pattern of the fallen runes. Some runes will be closer together than others—as one might expect, these runes will have the most direct influence on one another. Take the complete picture—divine each rune, but only in terms of where it fits into the broader pattern.

MURKSTAVES—THE RUNE COMES OUT UPSIDE DOWN

A rune may appear upside down on occasion. It may be face down rather than face up at times. The rune may come out facing sideways or at an odd angle in some situations, particularly when the runes are tossed. Because their significance is more indirect, these occurrences are known as "murk" staves. Some readers interpret an upside down rune's meaning as the opposite of the rune's meaning; in this case, the rune is read similarly to the tarot. On the other hand, a rune facing down can be interpreted as the polar opposite of its usual meaning.

However, another viewpoint to consider is that the runes, regardless of their appearance, imply what they imply. In other words, Uruz represents the Aurochs and its might, irrespective of how it appears during the reading. What counts is where it falls in the rune cast; for example, if it's closest to sowilu, which means sun or victory, uruz may imply having the strength to achieve that win.

The rune caster must ultimately decide how they feel about the runes and their placement in each given casting. For the best results, I recommend picking one strategy and sticking to it.

Chapter 10: Heathen Rituals—What Do You Need

The way heathens worship and perform rituals varies widely, depending on who they are and which groups they belong. These practices also vary from one group of the same religion to another. At the same time, some might be fairly traditional in their beliefs. For example, others may follow a more modern type of ritual passed down through generations or adapted after interactions with other religions.

A person needs to be wearing an Asatru symbol if they want to worship Norse gods. This can either be a necklace or something like Thor's Hammer worn on their clothing, chest, arm, etc. Fire is also needed for worshiping the deities because it provides light and warmth during ceremonies and the ceremonial cleansing of ritual tools. The next necessary item required in Asatru worship is altars, which can be any flat surface used by worshippers. Invocations spoken during Asatru rituals include "Hail" and "Heil." Places ideal for worship depend upon what type of setting you desire: outdoor locations with natural beauty work best, but indoor settings also work depending on what you're looking for.

Asatru Symbol

All Norse religions are grounded in the natural world, and they celebrate their gods through nature. So wearing an Asatru symbol is a way to show your faith in Thor or Odin by showing them that you respect all of creation. This follows how these religions believe everything has its spirit and should be treated with reverence because it can bring good things into someone's life if we treat it well first! But even though many people wear symbols like hammers and runes on leather bracelets as jewelry, others opt to create more intricate pieces such as actual hammer pendants so the entire piece will speak volumes about what kind of person they want other Pagans to know them to be.

FIRE

Asatru is a faith that worships the gods of Norse and Germanic legend. Fire plays such an important role in worship because it was thought to be holy by these people, who viewed flame as not just something for warmth or light but also spirituality and purification. A ceremony would typically start with lighting fires on either side of the altar before entreating Odin's presence through prayers from ancient texts like Havamal (sayings). This passage connects divinity with earthly life; our ancestors believed they could only reach God if their souls were pure after being cleansed through the fire, so ceremonies involved burning offerings made up of foodstuffs considered unworthy for consumption: parts discarded from otherwise edible animals sacrificed at various points during festivities.

ALTARS

Our altar and shrine have to be at eye level with nature, which is crucial when worshiping the gods in this earth-based religion. Therefore, Asatru altars are usually made of natural materials such as wood or stone that can withstand weather conditions without deteriorating as plastic would under harsh conditions. The top surface may also include a fire bowl, so we have light offerings during nighttime ceremonies while there are no artificial lights around us except from sources far away.

Altars are made of many materials, but the most important material is wood. Wood has a natural energy that helps to heighten and promote spiritual connections for worshippers. An altar can come from many different materials like bricks or metal. Still, one type that seems particularly fitting is wooden ones because they strongly connect with nature's energies!

INCANTATIONS AND CONVERSATIONS

Incantations are spoken words used in many religions to help us connect with the divine. For example, in Asatru, we use chants for various purposes, including calling forth a deity, appeasing an angry spirit, or helping out when someone is having trouble during their rites and rituals.

Some examples are "Hail Thor!" which is what followers say whenever they feel like he's been forgotten; "Yggdrasil," which means "World Tree"; and finally, "I call upon all deities" to summon other gods into our circle if one isn't present yet!

LOCATION

Certain ancient Norse beliefs such as Asatru are still practiced today, but not without criticism. The practitioners of this religion need to find the appropriate space and time for worship that is free from obstruction by others in society. It would be ideal if they can do so at a private location where noise pollution will also be minimalized or eliminated. Typically, these places include homes with backyards or woodlands that afford privacy and silence to enhance spiritual experience during rituals like blot, which includes offerings given up on behalf of those who have died peacefully as an Asatruar.

A good place for your next gathering with other followers of Norse tradition can be a natural setting. Whether in an awe-inspiring location, like Red Rocks Park near Denver or Yosemite National Park just outside San Francisco, or at home by building up and decorating a simple outdoor altar space using branches from trees and stones you find on site.

There is no wrong way to practice as long as it's done respectfully with consideration given not only to yourself but those nearby who may have differing beliefs about what should happen there that day too. If possible, try meditating before entering this sacred ground so they know why you're coming into their sanctuary; if unable, make sure when departing that both parties have been honored for what was done there that day. Heathen rituals are frequently divided into two types: Blót and Sumble.

Blót

A traditional heathen ritual can be described as a "blót" or an offering to the gods, at which time they bless their followers with good luck in exchange for some sacrifice from them.

Conversely, it is also said that when someone offers themselves up entirely without any expectation of reward (as was done by Jesus on the cross), this will constitute a sumble instead, giving all you have so your god may keep blessing those around you.

Blót is the term for animal sacrifice in heathen traditions. This kind of ritual was used to form long-lasting relationships with gods, ancestors or landvaettir since they require some exchange (in this case, an offering). Offerings can be anything from food to drink to currency, but what festivals are known for most often are animal offerings, typically cooked before being eaten by ceremony participants. The word blót derives from blood, meaning that these rituals were exclusively about sacrificing animals. At the same time, other practices, such as votive offerings, where gifts are given without any expectation of compensation, would fall under the scheme instead.

Sumble

Sumble is the term for a heathen ceremony which is about building relationships within the community itself. These sumbles are, more often than not, relatively informal. They can be any gathering of people who share mutual interests where no one leader is presiding over them or overseeing what happens. The word derives from Old Norse words meaning "to build" and "together." They happen to reinforce shared values among participants that transcend religious differences such as language barriers, since these gatherings usually include native English speakers and Swedish immigrants living together.

These ceremonies are often seen as ways to build relationships with one another within the community. They can involve sharing food or drink, having some competition (especially when involving children), making decisions about a common issue, practicing divination, healing rituals or even storytelling. Unlike blót, an exchange where someone offers something for their god/ancestor/landvaettir, getting back what they offer plus more, a sumble is giving without expecting anything in return.

In a sumble, there are typically at least three rounds. The first goes to the gods and goddesses, whom we honor with our rituals year-round. In the second round of drinking, from an open horn passed around by all participants, in turn, toast your ancestors and deceased heroes. Finally, the third is reserved as "open."

In a sumble ritual performed during Beltane festivals across Europe today, honoring fertility deities such as Freya or Matronae Aufaniae, among others, it's customary to toast the Earth Mother and start a dance that will bring energy into her womb.

In heathen culture, it is believed that sumble rituals are used more to build relationships within communities than blót, which tends toward sacrificing animals or offerings to develop long-term relationships with gods/ancestors.

Blóts tend to be much more ceremonial, while sumbles focus on storytelling. It's not uncommon for these sorts of ceremonies to involve ritual nudity (although this happens less often nowadays). A typical blót performed by a heathen today would include an offering such as food, incense, candles, and wine or mead, among other things, depending on the form the blót takes.

Sumble rituals are typically more about storytelling and the exchange of gifts, a sort of ritualized party to celebrate community life. In today's sumbles, one would prepare an offering such as food; wine or mead might also be included, depending on the form the sumble takes.

In both cases, these offerings tend to be given so that relationships can grow between gods/ancestors and people - not just for our benefit, but because they believe it's healthy for them too!

During this time, the Earth Mother is honored with prayers and offerings, while old family stories are shared to keep the lore alive.

Create Your Rituals: Four Factors to Consider

You'll eventually reach a point where you'll need to write and officiate your ritual. Don't be alarmed. It happens to everyone.

Below I list four essential factors to know and organize before you start your rituals.

Know Your Audience

A ritual in your living room with you and five of your kindred mates is one thing. However, what if it's going to be a more significant event outside or on the go? It might not work out so well for those who can't come near the fire as they'll need an alternative way to connect and feel involved.

Know that when hosting any ritual at home, there are some things you need to remember: first off, know your audience—if this is just another night inside or around the fireplace with only six people, then great! But what about rituals where more people are involved?

It's essential to make sure that everyone is on board with the ritual before you start. Some practices are so open and free-form, anyone can walk in at any time! Sometimes this presents a problem because people might not understand what they're doing or why they're there. You may need to spend some time explaining the significance of your activity for it to go smoothly; otherwise, someone might leave mid-ritual, whereas you want everyone involved as much as possible.

To do so, make sure to set the stage for ritual by making it a time of reverence and openness.

It's also important to keep in mind that any activity you're doing, no matter how small or large is a form of communication with the spiritual world. So take care to be mindful when choosing activities and their meaning.

Suppose you're dealing with a "mixed bag" of heathens and non-heathens. In that case, it's a good idea to think of the ceremony in terms of "speaking the same language." In other words, you may need to conduct things a bit differently than you would at home so that everyone can understand what's going on. You may also need to explain a bit more than you would for a group of all-heathens.

HOW MANY PEOPLE ARE COMING?

If you're looking for a fun way to get everyone in the group connected, officiating a ritual is perfect. The larger your group, the more effort it'll take on behalf of whoever's leading things. However, this can also mean more chances for people to find common ground and create sacred space with unified efforts.

Children are powerful forces. If they come to your ritual, be prepared for the possibility of them running wild and taking over—and also design with all-ages activities!

The young ones attending rituals can steal everyone's attention away from being cute or naughty, so if you're hosting a ceremony with children in attendance, ask how old they are so you know what type of behavior to expect from them beforehand.

The more people who attend your ritual, the longer it will take.

There are many factors to keep in mind when working with large groups of participants for a ritual experience. One consideration is that as more and more attendees arrive, they'll make their way through space until there's no room left. This can result in instability or discomfort among some individuals seeking isolation (e.g., introverts) and over-saturation of stimulation (loud music or noise) during breaks between activities.

WHERE ARE YOU HOLDING THE RITUAL?

If you're having a blót in the living room, you can only welcome as many people as the room can comfortably contain; if it's too crowded, the atmosphere may become more about "not elbowing your neighbor," which can detract from the ritual. On the other hand, if you hold your ceremony outside, you will need to raise your voice to be heard, as you will have more space.

Do You Have All the Ritual Tools Needed?

Ideally, it would help if you had all your ritual tools on hand before beginning. But, if not, conducting a brief moment of preparation can help ensure that the procedure goes smoothly and according to plan.

For example, when first performing a new spell or amulet consecration ceremony for yourself or someone else who needs healing energy from within themselves, you must make sure you have everything required before starting. This includes whatever offerings might be part of the ritual. An example could be grain, wood carvings, mead, vegetables, etc., and any necessary ceremonial items like blades and amulets, natural materials, wool yarn or animal skin, fabrics, etc.

Ritual Roles and Ritual Participation

Now that you have read about the important things to check before running the ritual. Let's dive into the details of an excellent blót.

One uses a single officiant, who takes on all of the responsibilities during the rite. While this results in a simple, well-coordinated ritual, it also decreases the amount of active participation. If more than one person shares the ritual framework, the duties must be defined so that everyone has a chance to participate. Furthermore, heathen rites are typically participative, implying that everyone present will have a minor, personal role. Despite this, a focused core is still required. This means that no matter how many "assistants" you have, one clear officiant should be present.

The blót should be designed clearly around its central purpose. If, for instance, you decide to write a blót to Thor, thanking him for protecting Midgard, then everything should orbit that. You need to focus on the theme of the blót.

Some people use their own words to deliver the blót, while others memorize and recite verses from the Poetic Edda.

Some prefer using a book with precise wording to deliver speeches or perform ritualistic ceremonies like "The Voluspa."

When you are executing a ritual, the plan will inevitably evolve. You may think your ritual's life ends when you've written about everything on paper. Still, as soon as people interact with it and add their ideas, they'll see just how majestic and holy an experience can be. No two rituals are ever alike!

When you execute any spiritual ceremony, there will inevitably be changes in the way things go down. A blot has been designed explicitly by all involved parties before execution, so everyone knows what it needs at every stage. However, once participants have interacted with it or added something new during the practice, these events become much more individual, and there is a solid personal connection with the ritual.

Just as no two rituals are the same, rituals differ in their outcomes too. This is what makes these ceremonies such a powerful experience. You never know how it will turn out, and that's why magic exists.

DESIGNING YOUR IDEAL BLÓT

Any ceremony, regardless of tradition, religion, or folklore, usually comprises the following elements:

Sacred space creation
Invocation
Blessing of the offering
The ritual's focal point, attention and performance of the offering
Sacred space is closed

Rituals are deeply personal to each participant and should be as unique as each person can make it. One way of ensuring the ceremony is successful is by taking care of what gifts people offer at these events - some appropriate examples might be food, drink, money donations, etc.

We have to remember our ancestors gave just the best they could to these rituals, and we should honor them the same way, with greatness.

Most of your planning time should be focused on the ritual's focal point. You should spend most of your creative and holy efforts constructing the "primary focus" for the ritual. It is crucial to devote your creative energy and time to craft the most significant part of it. This will be where you put all of your creativity because it plays an integral role in determining how engaging people find it.

The following are some tricks of the trade used by heathens while writing blóts and other rites.

KENNINGS, ALLITERATION, AND BYNAMES

A kenning is a metaphor, often a compound noun used in place of something more familiar. The word kenning stems from the Old Norse root and means "to know" or "to understand." A famous example of this kind of figurative language is Beowulf's use of "sea-girt land" to refer to the coast of Denmark.

A kenning can also be a compound adjective, such as "shield-fingered" or "thronged with sorrow."

Some examples of kennings:

- Ankle biter = a very young child.
- Bean counter = a bookkeeper or accountant.
- Bookworm = someone who reads a lot.
- Brown noser = a person who does anything to gain approval.

There is a difference between kennings and bynames, which have to be considered as nicknames. Freya, for example, can be referred to as Horn, Syr, and Mardoll. These are all bynames or nicknames.

Alliteration was another tactic used by our forefathers before Christianity.

Alliteration is an effect created when words at the beginning and end of sentences start with similar sounds.

The word alliteration comes from the Latin meaning "to repeat." It often occurs throughout Beowulf, where it creates a poetic sound that reflects the old Norse language's emphasis on sonic values.

With this technique, you repeat the same sound in different words throughout an entire sentence or paragraph—that's all it takes!

Alliteration is great for adding flair to any piece of text, even more to your ritual. In addition, alliterations are usually seen as exciting because they have many qualities: repetition, variety, continuity; the list goes on!

Consonant alliteration is a form of repetition that sounds pleasing to the ear. It usually occurs in English by lining up words with their first consonants, but it can also happen at other points during your speech. When used wisely and sparingly, this technique could make any ritual much more interesting for everybody!

Analyze these sentences to see some examples of alliteration.

- **Becky's b**eagle **b**arked and **b**ayed, **b**ecoming **b**othersome for **B**illy.

- **C**an you **k**eep the **c**at from **c**lawing the **c**ouch? It's **c**reating **c**haos.

- **Dan's d**og **d**ove **d**eep in the **d**am, **d**rinking **d**irty water as he **dove**.

- **Fred's** friends fried fritters for **Friday's** food.

Chapter 11: Heathen Holidays and Festivals

Celebrations and festivals are an integral part of heathenism, with the calendar being filled to the brim with holidays. There is a feast day for every occasion!

Heathens celebrate through rituals and feasting at home and in local temples or outdoors on open grounds. Celebrating special occasions often goes beyond food and involves activities such as playing games while eating.

Here are some of the most important festivals and holidays on the Heathen calendar.

One of an Asatruar's primary responsibilities is to go out and perform at festivals. Whether it's to appease or honor gods, goddesses, ancestors, and other divine entities or in remembrance of loved ones who have passed on from this world into Valhalla, there are many different reasons, personal to each practitioner.

Norse and Germanic tribes celebrated different holidays every year, so Asatru has a compilation of all the feasts that were considered necessary throughout Northern Europe.

Here is a list of some of the most important ones.

Yule or Yuletide – The 12-Day Festival

The Festival of Yule starts approximately on December 20th (early morning) and goes until the beginning of the following year. If you are a fan of the ancient Scandinavian pagan tradition, this will be your favorite time with your family and friends.

No other time is as sacred as Yuletide because it marks the return of Baldr from Helheim. Initially celebrated by all ancient Germanic tribes, it was considered one of their most solemn events.

Yule or Yuletide is a 12-day festival celebrating the winter solstice. It is a time to celebrate family, fellowship, and games.

On the first day of Yuletide, we honor our mothers and those who came before them. We celebrate their legacy by thanking Frigga and other ancestral spirits called Disir.

The first night of Yuletide (Mother's Night) is about reverencing Frigga and Disirs - female ancestral spirit guards that manifest themselves during this festive season. They typically appear with their children or grandchildren around them sometime between November 1st and December 12th every year!

DISTING

The Disting, or Disablot, festival is celebrated in Sweden to honor the first public assembly of the year. It's also referred to as Charming of the Plow, and it takes place at the end of January.

As the Disting festival approaches, Danes prepare for new beginnings by praying to their gods and furrowing the fields. A solemn tradition that marks a time of beginning. Danes worship their gods and lots as the Disting festival approaches.

OSTARA (MARCH 20TH–21ST)

Ostara, or the spring equinox, is a time for celebration as we welcome the warmer months. Celebrated on March 21st every year to mark when night equals day (a total of 24 hours), Ostara can be traced back to many cultures, including Germanic tribes. During this festival, Germans will sacrifice goats.

The festival is named after the goddess Ostara. She was primarily worshiped by the Teutonic tribes, where she represented new beginnings and promised prosperity if properly honored at the start of each season.

The Ostara festival is a celebration of the revival of nature after months and months of winter. Home decorations typically include flowers, colored eggs, budding trees, boughs, etc. Still, many people use more than just these items to make their exterior homes look even better for this event.

Walpurgis Night or May Eve (April 30th–May Day)

Walpurgis, the most important day for witches and wizards in Scandinavia, is celebrated by casting spells to find love. In Finland, they also try their luck with a game of dice or cards called Wirntaja.

Walpurgisnacht, otherwise known as the Witch's Night, falls on April 30th. To celebrate, people light bonfires and gather around them, singing songs to ward off evil spirits.

The May Tree is taken out in a procession during the Festival of Walpurgis. Because Walpurgis is the Germanic counterpart of Valentine's Day, and Freya is the goddess of love and witchcraft, heathens think Freya is the goddess to be celebrated during this festival. Therefore, during this celebration in Scandinavia, the May Tree is carried out in a parade.

Midsummer – Summer Solstice (June 20th–21st)

Midsummer is a religious celebration for heathens that takes place on the summer solstice. Midsummer's Eve, which falls on either June 20th or 21st, is believed to be one of the two most critical Germanic festivals after Yuletide.

The midsummer tradition celebrates life and light with customs like bonfires and singing songs to keep evil spirits at bay during this time.

On Midsummer's Night, celebrations include bonfires and singing. The tradition of dancing around a pole is also followed enthusiastically by many people who believe that it will bring good luck to those involved. Lastly, speeches are made about how beautiful nature can be on this day or about whatever topic any speaker desires to cover related to the celebration.

The long, hot days of summer provide a time to celebrate life and prosperity. Midsummer is the apex of our year, but it is also the death of Baldr, the god of sunshine and happiness. From this time onward, we will inch closer towards winter's cold grasp with every passing day.

FREYFEST OR LAMMAS OR LITHASBLOT (JULY 31ST–AUGUST 1ST)

Lammas is thought to be an Anglicized version of the heathen festival of thankfulness for bread known as "hlaf-mass" or "loaves festival." Heathens commemorate Freyr's birthday by baking bread in the shape and likeness of the god, which is subsequently offered and consumed. The first fruits of the harvest arrive on August 1st, and the first sheaf is offered to the heathen gods during Thanksgiving in Germanic traditions.

Lammas is a time to give thanks for the bounty of grain, fruit and vegetables before winter comes. It's also called Lithasblot or Freyfest as it honors Freyr and Sif - Thor's wives, with long golden hair representing the fields ripe for harvest.

Harvestfest or Winter Nights (October 31st)

The end of the harvest season may not seem like a big deal to some, but this day is celebrated as the last chance for industrious farmers and hunters before winter arrives. In addition, it's a tradition on this day to butcher animals that are too old or weak for the harsh winters ahead.

The festival is also referred to as Frey-Blessing, Dis-Blessing, and Elf-Blessing. It is time to pay homage to the land spirits, ancestral spirits, and Vanir gods.

It is the first day of winter. It was a time when everyone was supposed to focus their gaze inward rather than outward. According to Norse legend, the housewife oversaw winter night celebrations, and the last sheaf was left in the fields for the gods, spirits, and deities.

The Winter Nights feast was commemorated by recounting historical legends of bravery and triumph and emphasizing future successes. The Harvestfest honored the power, respect, and significance of our forefathers and mothers. It also reminded people of a critical aspect of Germanic belief: death was neither fearful nor wicked. Death was not as significant an issue to consider for the Nordic people as living and dying with dignity was.

Chapter 12: The Contemporary Asatruar

Many people have questions about the Asatru faith and how to keep it strong. From figuring out what that means in today's world to practicing rituals correctly, there are many ways you can do to persevere on your path as an Asatruar.

Although Asatru is often seen as an old-time religion, it has grown exponentially in recent years. Now, people from all walks of life practice many different variations of this faith around the globe.

This chapter will present various steps to become a modern-day Asatruar and connect with other faith practitioners. The intent here is not necessarily to provide complex rules but rather guidelines, so interested people may find it easier to explore their connection with this ancient Norse religion and others like them worldwide.

Many practitioners of Asatru walk a long path with uncertainties, like struggling through doubts, questioning if one is doing things right enough, or wondering where they fit into society as outsiders looking for spiritual guidance outside their existing cultural identity.

Modern-day Asatru is practiced in various ways, so it may be challenging to know where to start. But before embarking on this journey, you must decide what type of contemporary Asatruar you will be. A practitioner but not necessarily someone who wants to connect with others through social media sites or other means? Just reading about this faith and looking for information on how things can work in both practice and spirituality contentment while remaining solitary practitioners (regardless if they live alone or not)? Or seeking out community building and a sense of belonging to something, which may come from joining the group or social media.

All three levels of involvement are critical in different ways and should not be disregarded. Those looking for information about how things work can find it here, but they would also do well using other knowledge sources if they want more out of their spiritual journey. However, those seeking community connection and someone with whom they can share their thoughts and feelings will often look at these pages with disdain because all one finds is cold data rather than sharing an experience with others like themselves in real life.

FOLLOW ASATRU IN FIVE STEPS

1 - LISTEN AND CONVERSE TO YOUR GODS

When you feel called to follow Norse paganism, the first thing you should do is listen and converse to your gods. Remember that gods are your friends and kinsfolk in heathenism, and chatting with them can help you create rapport and comprehend what you need to accomplish and how to proceed.

Early on in your journey, you must develop the practice of conversing with your gods. Unfortunately, we are so preoccupied with business and social pursuits that we neglect to talk with our gods in modern life. However, like other habits such as eating healthily, exercising, and so on, if you persist in developing this habit, it may and will become a part of your daily routine.

2 - Discover and learn about Asatru ancestors

The second step of your Asatru path is to gather knowledge and insight. As you discover more about your Viking and Germanic forebears, you'll find yourself unlearning many of the things that were unintentionally or intentionally included in the history of the Nordic people. Remind yourself that the Germanic tribes' forefathers were highly evolved and intelligent, capable of building fast-moving boats, and great fighters. They traveled enormous distances, conquered many places, and assimilated the conquered lands' culture and traditions. If our forefathers had merely been savages or fools, they would not have accomplished so much.

Your faith will grow stronger as you discover more about Nordic ancestors and ancient tribes. Re-reading and researching the books, poetry, and prose you've been reading and studying is a terrific method to expand your knowledge of Norse paganism. You could also see whether translating your lectures into a different language can assist you. This practice will improve your language skills and help you gain a better understanding of Norse wisdom, mythology, and ancient, forgotten knowledge.

3 - Give offerings to gods

The third step is to present offerings to the gods. Gifts of all sorts are meant to empower the gods, and this is why you must participate in giving offerings. By participating in gift exchanges, we can empower both ourselves and our deities when they need us most. It's time for everyone who wants to become a practicing Heathen - or just an interested observer of Norse Paganism-to start understanding what these gifts entail and how they will benefit their lives greatly by offering them up properly!

There are many gods in the world, each with its likes and dislikes. For example, Odin is one of these deities who only drinks and never eats; if you offer him anything to eat or drink other than mead, he will be disappointed, making it unlikely that he'll help you out when needed. By studying Asatru beliefs such as this one, we can better understand how different pantheons work so we know what gifts they prefer - like, for example, knowing whether a god would rather have food offerings (Odin) or libations (Njord).

Start by making sacrifices in small basins. Then, write your own sacred words and seek their blessings. When you have finished that, don't forget to speak with them and ask about their reactions to all of these services - they are constantly sending messages through various forms and other people around you.

4 - CONNECT WITH ASATRUARS IN A COMMUNITY

The fourth step is to meet fellow Asatruars in person, join a kindred or attend an event.

Connecting with others who share your beliefs can be very fulfilling and inspiring. While it might not always feel like you're getting the spiritual satisfaction you need by yourself, being able to discuss sacred concepts with someone else is essential for that aspect of practice - so find people you click with!

Attending events such as religious services, workshops on traditional living skills (such as spinning wool), and conferences are also great ways to keep up on modern Asatru practices while meeting new friends and fellow pagans. In addition, people often "come out" at these sorts of gatherings which means they'll have plenty of company when making their personal revelations about what this religion truly brought into their lives.

5 - Have fun living the Asatru lifestyle

The fifth and most important step is to enjoy life as an Asatruar. In the end, it is crucial to keep in mind that while you may be a modern-day Asatruar, you'll never truly know this religion until you live it. You can't just read about these traditions and hope they will speak to your soul; feeling connected with Thor on a spiritual level requires physically engaging with him through daily rites like using consecrated items for worship or drawing runes during meditation.

It's really up to each individual how much of their life they want to devote towards practicing their faith. Still, we all agree that being an active participant in our spirituality always leads to enlightenment (whether it's intellectual, emotional, or both). It shouldn't feel like hard work: you should always have a sense of fulfillment in doing meaningful things in your life.

Getting in touch with fellow Asatruars

We know that it can be challenging to find other Astruars in your area. You may want to check places, such as libraries and bookstores, which are more likely than not going to contain people with similar interests or beliefs. If the Internet is still accessible for you, then we recommend using social media sites like Facebook for finding friends who share your faith - but if this doesn't work, there's always old-fashioned word of mouth!

Please make contact with like-minded people in your local area and connect with them. Most of these people will know how to assist you in developing your unique heathen connection. Here are some pointers to get you started:

- Use several search engines to look for the words "Asatru/kindred/Heathen, [your city name]" on the Internet.

Such searches are likely to provide some results, such as names, phone numbers, and addresses. So you can start with this foundational information.

• Look for Asatru links on social media platforms. Most of the big social media sites offer a dedicated page for several similar organizations.

• One of the premium apps that connects you with other believers can help you start a local meetup group. Although you may have to spend money, your efforts may be worthwhile. Even so, you should only utilize this if the other attempts have failed.

• Get in touch with other Pagan believers in your area, like Wiccans, for another option to contact Heathens. Given that many heathens begin their Asatru journey with Wiccan ideas, these ties are likely to put you in touch with Asatruars who are currently practicing.

KINDRED COMMUNITIES

There are plenty of perfect pagans out there to get you on the right track in your Asatru journey. They can offer connections, learnings, and fellowship for anyone looking!

One of the best ways to find a community that aligns with your spiritual beliefs is by looking for existing pagan communities. There are recognized and already established ones, such as The Troth or Asatru Belief Community USA (ABCUSA), which have memberships nationwide so you can easily connect to people personally even if they're across different states!

Here's a short list:

- Northern Mist Kindred
- Kenaz Kindred
- Shieldwall Kindred
- Northern Pines Heathen Kindred
- Hammerstone Kindred
- Oath Keepers Kindred
- Northern Rune Kindred
- Wyrd Ways Kindred
- Ulfr a Aesir Kindred
- Hrafn and Ulfr Kindred
- Laeradr

There are several pagan communities that you can contact for connections, learnings, and fellowship in your Asatru journey. Some groups may even have web pages dedicated to connecting people with those who share their beliefs, so if you do not see any on Facebook or other social media sites, try Google!

It's important to remember that you don't have to be a part of a group or community to be an Asatruar. You can practice and perform blót and other rites on your own. If you decide to go out and find a group to practice with, don't stay too long if you don't like them. It can be isolating to be the only Asatuar in a room, but it is critical that the individuals with whom you practice are decent, honest, and sincere.

Chapter 13: Performing a Blot

As we have already discussed in Chapter 9, a blot is a ceremony that can be performed for different purposes. The most common type of blot is to honor the Norse gods, but there are other types of rituals that celebrate the harvest or give thanks for a blessing received. For a better understanding of this ceremony, we will outline a communal blot dedicated to the goddess Frigga including preparations and performance complete with dialogues and actions, a solitary blot, and The Hammer Rite.

There are many different paths that one can take during their spiritual journey and it is important to find the right resources for you. One way that you can choose to explore your spirituality is through the pagan religion.

You will want to start by purifying yourself before performing any ritual or ceremony so it may be necessary for you to take a bath beforehand. In order to prepare for this type of spiritual journey, one should also create an altar space in their home where they will conduct rituals and ceremonies including items needed for the ritual. It is also recommended that an after-ritual activity like sharing be conducted to reinforce the outcome sought by the ceremony.

A Communal Blot to Frigga

First of all, we must recall who Frigga is and what objects or gifts are most precious to her. We are aware she is the highest-ranking Aesir goddess. In this particular blot, we will invoke

Frigga to share her gift in maintaining peace in our homes, following her example. This purpose will dictate the outcome of this blot. Another thing to consider would be the number of participants, which in this case is twelve adults. The location is the living room of a participant's home.

Now that we have determined the purpose and participants, it's time to gather the items we will need for the ritual. It is most helpful to outline the blot as if doing a script for a play.

Purpose/Outcome

As the goddess Frigga is in charge with the keeping of the house and all things within, we invoke Frigga's gift in maintaining frith in our homes.

Participants

12 adult attendees including officiant (godhi or gythja)

Location

Living room

Items required

Altar - a large table to hold all ritual items

Cloth - grandmother's linen tablecloth to cover the altar

Offering bowl - salad bowl inherited from grandmother

Representation of Frigga - Frigga's statue (antique keys or household keys will do in case statue is unavailable)

Mead - apple cider

Drinking vessel - heirloom glass from great aunt

Any other gifts or offerings for Frigga

Creation of Sacred Space

Place the altar in the middle of the room. Offerings are laid on the altar before beginning the ritual. Gather attendees around the altar. To begin, the officiant will ask everyone to take a deep breath and to focus their minds on the outcome of the blot - invoke Frigga's gift in maintaining frith or peace in the homes of those present.

Officiant: (stands facing the north) Before there was time, before the stars were in their places, there was a land, Niflheim hight. It was an icy and frozen land. The vast well Hvergelmir roiled within it, and frigid waters sprang from this seething well, forming rivers that flowed all over the place. (turns to face the south) Another land, Muspelheim hight, existed at the time. It was a world of fire, molten and aflame. Muspelheim spewed earth-made magma. (stands in the center facing either east or west) Between these lands was a mighty chasm known as Ginnungagap, a place brimming with roaring potential. Rivers poured into the gap from the north, and magma poured in from the south. When they came together deep within Ginnungagap, a great hiss of steam rose, and as it cleared, the great ash,

Yggdrasil, rose, its roots entwined with everything underground and its branches reaching ever upward and over, protecting all the worlds. It was here, in Ginnungagap, in the shadow of Yggdrasil, that the waters of Niflheim and the fires of Muspelheim collided, forming the rime that would become our earth. We find ourselves in sacred Midgard, the nexus of all things.

Invocation

Only Frigga (the honored deity) will be called to set the focus on the outcome of the blot. Everyone should think about Frigga and what she represents to the participant and the group gathered.

Officiant: (looking directly on Frigga's representation on the altar) Keeper of keys, mistress of Fensalir, beloved goddess, we call to you. We hold this blót today in your honor, wife of Odin, and we ask that you be present and witness us. Weaver who waits, seeress who sees but never speaks, lady of Asgard, we call to you. Hail Frigga.

Attendees: Hail!

(Officiant offers a small drink or grain, then places it into the offering bowl)

Blessing of the offerings

Officiant: (fills the drinking vessel with cider, lifts it up, and makes the sign of the of the hammer over its top) Blessed boon of bees, bountiful brew of Aegir, blood of Kvasir. May this mead carry our words from here into the Well of Wyrd, where they will reside forever (gives the vessel to the assigned participant).

Officiant: (faces the altar) Frigga, these offerings are gathered here for you. See them and know of our respect and love for you, Lady of Fensalir. Bless them, as they are yours.

Central Point/Focus of the Ritual

Officiant: Beloved of Odin, mother of Baldur, we call to you now. Times are troubled, and we notice strife even in our homes, and amongst the community. Weaver of linen, seeress, mistress of Fensalir, we make these offerings this day so that you may guide us. Help us to maintain the frithbonds between us, that we might remember all the good we are to one another. Help us soothe the social waters, so that strife may fade away. Help us by continuing to be an example for us, that your ability to maintain frith among the gods will prove the ways we maintain frith with one another, and in our homes. Let the inviolable peace reign, and may your wisdom guide us. (faces the altar and places hand over it) Glad gifts are given rest on your good altar. Accept these as our gratitude for your continued assistance to us. We offer them your honor. (motions for the drinking vessel and raises it high) Now we drink our toasts to you, keeper of keys. We raise this in your honor, and speak over the horn, that our words might reach your ears (passes it to the nearest participant).

Each participant will now say their prayers to the goddess when the vessel is received. Once done, the group should echo "Hail!" and the person holding the vessel should take a drink.

Officiant: (receives the vessel, says prayers and thanks, and places hand over it) Wealful words have been whispered over the waters of the Well, where they will form their own layer in wyrd. Wishes offered, thanks given, we share this drink now with Frigga (pours the remaining cider into the bowl and places the vessel aside).

Officiant: (raises hand over the items on the altar) Frigga, keeper of keys, wielder of wisdom, we ask that you bless this altar and all items on it. They will be physical representations of the frith we have asked you to share with us this day. Hail Frigga.

Attendees: Hail!

Closing of Sacred Space

Officiant: Offerings have been made, words have been spoken. Frigga, we thank you for your many gifts to us, and especially for helping us maintain frith in our homes and community.

Officiant: Well have we offered, and well have we thanked. We libate now to Frigga, who we honor here today. Hail Frigga.

Attendees: Hail!

This ends the ritual. A meal could be shared together thereafter to maintain the frith, the blot's purpose.

A Solitary Blot for Frigga

Blot is founded on building and maintaining community relationships, and a community of one cannot survive. However, it's possible that there aren't any other heathens in your region or that you're new to Asatru and haven't yet made any local community connections. Individual spiritual connections to the gods, ancestors, and local house or land spirits are also strengthened inside the home. Solitary blóts are typically more basic than community-led blóts, yet they are just as meaningful. There is no need for spoken words, and heartfelt prayers are acceptable.

Mead and ale are the most traditional offerings, but your favorite drink is suitable, too. What's important is that the offering will delight Frigga. Do not choose a gift that you personally dislike, making the item your reject. Be in your best behavior and do not be rude.

Stand in front of your altar or near a tree in nature. Remove the cap from the beverage. Take some time to think about what you want to get out of the offering. Concentrate on what you know about Frigga and how you want to connect with her or appreciate her for her gifts.

Once you have concentrated on these things and felt it is time in your heart, raise the drink in a quiet toast. Take a sip, then pour the remaining into an offering bowl or right at the tree's roots to share. Pause for another moment to thank Frigga before walking away. The ceremony has come to an end. If you're in an apartment or somewhere else where you can't get outside, keep the offering in the bowl for at least half an hour to allow Frigga to absorb the essence of the offering, then pour the contents down a drain.

THE HAMMER RITE

This is a quick cleansing and clearing of space ceremony. I , it is a recent invention that closely resembles the Pentagram's Lesser Banishing Ceremony, a ritual established in the early twentieth century that involves calling out to the directions to conjure guardian spirits and create sacred space, in both form and intent. Many modern heathens use this as a starting point for their rituals, while others do not. Even so, it's a good method to clear and create sacred space.

Officiant: (with a ritual hammer or hands raised to the skies) Hammer in the north! Hallow and hold this holy stead! (make the sign of the hammer toward the north then turn to face the east) Hammer in the east! Hallow and hold this holy stead!(make the sign of the hammer toward the east then turn to face the south) Hammer in the south! Hallow and hold this holy stead! (make the sign of the hammer toward the south then turn to face the west) Hammer in the west! Hallow and hold this holy stead! (make the sign of the hammer toward the west then raise the hammer directly overhead) Hammer of Asgard! Hallow and hold this holy stead! (make the hammer sign overhead then hold the hammer toward the ground) Hammer of Midgard! Hallow and hold this holy stead!

Asatru, as heathens like to say, is spirituality with homework: if you want to be a modern heathen, you'll need to be creative. Nothing will appear in front of you and tell you what you should do. This can be both beneficial and detrimental. It can be beneficial since you have the opportunity to be yourself and develop your own brand of heathenism; but, it can also be detrimental because you may become disoriented. Find a close-knit group of friends and family to practice with when it comes to rituals. It doesn't matter if you're all beginners; you may work together to figure out the finest ways to create modern heathen rites. It will undoubtedly be a highly rewarding experience for everyone if we do so!

It is important to find resources and people that will guide you on your spiritual journey, but why? The answer lies in the importance of understanding how rituals work. A deeper knowledge can be gained by finding out about symbolism or structure.

People often rely solely upon their own experiences for guidance when they embark on a new spiritual path. However, it's never too late to start learning more about what other traditions have to offer; including symbols and structures found in various cultures around the world.

Well Done!

I hope you loved this book and found it worth your time. If so, I would be forever grateful if you could leave me a review on Amazon to help other readers find my work. The marketplaces are tough these days - which is why reviews really make a difference for authors like myself who want their published works seen by the masses! It only takes 30 seconds of your time but definitely makes an important impact in helping emerging writers get more attention from potential buyers out there looking for new books to read.

Thank you again for reading my book, happy reviewing!

In case you enjoyed the notions or learned something useful from what I shared, please post an honest review online visiting *https://swiy.io/AsatruReview* OR scan the QR code with your phone*:

above link is made for amazon.com. If you buy the book from other marketplaces, kindly leave us a review by visiting the review page in your respective marketplace. Thank you!

BONUS 1: FREE WORKBOOK - VALUE ~~12.99$~~

To help you take some time for yourself and reflect on what actions to take while reading the book, I have prepared a Free Workbook with some key questions to ask yourself and a To Do List which can help you get deeper into the topic of this book. I hope this helps!

You can find the Free Workbook by visiting

>> https://swiy.io/AsatruWB<<

OR scan the QR Code with your phone's camera

BONUS 2: FREE BOOK – VALUE $14.99

As a way of saying thank you for downloading this book, I'm offering the eBook *RUNES FOR BEGINNERS A Pagan Guide to Reading and Casting the Elder Futhark Rune Stones for Divination, Norse Magic and Modern Witchcraft* for FREE.

In *Runes for Beginners*, Melissa Gomes reveals some of the most interesting and secret aspects of how to perform Runes Reading and Runes Casting. You will discover new insights into the magical word of Runes and how to link with them.

Click Below for the Free Gift Or Scan the QR Code with your phone

>> https://swiy.io/RunesFree<<

Bonus 3: Free Audio Version of This Book

If you love listening to audiobooks on-the-go or would enjoy a narration as you read along, I have great news for you. You can download the audiobook version of **Asatru for Beginners** for FREE just by signing up for a FREE 30-day Audible trial!

Visit the website https://swiy.io/AsatruAudioBook OR scan the QR code with your phone:

Lightning Source UK Ltd.
Milton Keynes UK
UKHW02063528I021
392990UK00011B/679